# MAKING DECISIONS

BUSINESS & MANAGEMENT

# MAKING DECISIONS

## How to develop effective skills for making good decisions

**Dean Juniper**

**How To Books**

Cartoons by Mike Flanagan

**British Library Cataloguing in Publication Data**
A catalogue record for this book is available from the British Library.

© Copyright 1998 by Dean Juniper.

Published by How To Books Ltd, 3 Newtec Place,
Magdalen Road, Oxford OX4 1RE, United Kingdom.
Tel: (01865) 793806. Fax: (01865) 248780.
email: info@howtobooks.co.uk
www.howtobooks.co.uk

*Note:* The material contained in this book is set out in good faith for
general guidance and no liability can be accepted for loss or expense
incurred as a result of relying in particular circumstances on statements made
in the book. The law and regulations are complex and liable to change, and
readers should check the current position with the relevant authorities before
making personal arrangements.

Produced for How To Books by Deer Park Productions.
Typeset by PDQ Typesetting, Stoke-on-Trent, Staffs.
Printed and bound by Cromwell Press, Trowbridge, Wiltshire.

# Contents

# List of Illustrations

# Preface

The power to make and take decisions distinguishes humankind from the animal kingdom. It is a product of our hugely developed brain, which has significantly but not completely insulated itself from instinctively driven and controlled behaviour, putting actions under some conscious control, and making planning and anticipation the determinants of what is done.

And yet this unique, distinctive human power has seldom been examined psychologically, and what evaluation has been made has usually been of a superficial, unsystematic kind. More sinisterly, there have been and still are attempts to persuade humanity that its decisional powers are illusions; presumably to make easier the acceptance of the decisions of others. And, especially in the market world, tactics to capitalise on the powers of impulsive rather than reasoned choices seek to undermine the capability of consumers to judge needs and wants impartially.

Generally, it ought to be accepted as an axiom that the result of abandoning freedom of decision is not liberation. Decision is, in effect, highly diversible; we choose for ourselves, or have choices made for us, but decision there must be.

It therefore becomes essential that we focus on decision-making as a topic worthy of serious study. In this book we begin by identifying our personal decisional space, the degree of freedom we enjoy to make choices. Then we analyse the elements which go to make up a decision, and importance of aims and motivation, and the place of information. Factors facilitating decision and the role of risk-taking follow. Then we tackle the range of possible decisions, concentrating particularly on decisions not to decide, a very intriguing form of 'choice'. Throughout we maintain a watching brief on decisions related to marketing and human organisation in business settings. Finally we confront the issue of decisional responsibility: did we choose rightly?

This book is a self-instructional manual containing many

different training exercises: questionnaires, summaries, charts, assessment sheets, and a variety of personal histories and case studies. Except where I have provided items from my personal experience, all the narratives are fictional, and the characters in them do not exist.

*Dean Juniper*

# 1
# Understanding Decision-Making

## THE EXAMPLE OF T. E. LAWRENCE

In one of the climaxes of David Lean's epic film *Lawrence of Arabia*, Robert Boult, its scriptwriter, takes us to the aftermath of the capture of the Red Sea port of Akaba, and serves us a breathtaking scene. Akaba, reckoned by Lawrence's Bedouin chieftains to be impregnable, and defended on its landward side by a desert judged uncrossable, has fallen to a young British colonel. It is an unimaginable triumph for him, rendered all the sweeter by this successful flouting of age-old local experience by a desert amateur, to say nothing of his brilliant notion of attacking the Turkish fortress from the rear.

The Bedouin chieftains, excited by victory, come to eat humble pie, whenever this brash, confident, decisive, British adventurer is ready to serve it. With the screams and shots of the dying battle echoing in the background, Sheikh Auda, the spokesman, elegantly and reverentially admits how wrong he and his fellow sheikhs have been. 'El Aurens,' he says, simply, 'We have an Arab saying; for some men it is written, and they cannot escape their destiny. But for you, El Aurens, nothing is written, because you write it yourself.'

## A FRAMEWORK FOR DECISION-MAKING

Robert Boult's glorious testimony to decisive action cannot be bettered. It is an inspirational summons to a belief in free will as a guide to successful living, and a challenge to the doctrine that would have us devalue decision-making on the spurious grounds that our destiny is already mapped out for us.

But we need more than a summons, however inspirational, to give us confidence in our decision-making powers. Decision-making is a skill that can be developed or, more accurately, a set of choice-creating competencies and like any such ability must be tested and practised to gain mastery in it. Learning decision-making further requires a scheme of instruction, a framework on which the process can be built. This has to be simple, flexible and comprehensive, and it is just such a structure that forms the basis of this book.

The model we use consists of four components:

- Aims
- Information
- Evaluation
- Decision.

A **considered decision**, the only reliable mix of *choice* and *action*, is a product of all four components working together in harmony, each contributing essential input to the decisional outcome. Considered successful decisions are indeed a dynamic orchestration of these four themes, built from skills acquired or developed, and usually forming part of a personal tradition of well-judged choosing.

T. E. Lawrence was far from being a normal man, and his were far from normal times. Despite this, his extraordinary decision, about which we know so much and may still learn more, can most usefully illuminate the **aims**, **information**, **evaluation** and **decision** framework, and serve as our first case study. It is a dramatic and dramatised story demonstrating how fiction, as well as fact, have been skilfully fused in the Lawrence of Arabia saga. But this, if anything, increases its usefulness as a learning aid. We can use its colour and complexity to our modern advantage.

## SEEING LAWRENCE IN THE FRAMEWORK

### Aims
Lawrence's aims were multiple and complex. He was first and foremost a British Army officer committed to a guerilla war, a sideshow campaign against the Turkish Empire, with the objective of breaking up its communications. Sideshow though this might seem to the Army HQ in Cairo, Lawrence and his fellow officers intended to turn it into a decisive front, and by rousing local Arabs to revolt, destroy Turkish resistance.

Lawrence also had a vision of a united Arab nation, led by Palestinians, stretching from Damascus to Mecca. This was a pipe-dream, but it was not until the 1920s that he knew it was unrealisable.

And, of course, Lawrence sought glory, not an unreasonable

quest for the immensely gifted, bastard son of an Irish baronet. But when glory came, and his fame grew greater than any contemporary soldier in any army, Lawrence, ran away from it, and tried to bury himself in anonymity.

Lawrence's aims, then, were complex, being both short and long term. They also intertwined intricately with his motivation, being difficult to separate, and perhaps causally interdependent.

## Information
Lawrence had a wealth of information, some of it very recently acquired, such as the disposition of Turkish forces in and around the Arabian Desert, much of it derived from his pre-war, archaeological expeditions as a student/spy, when he prowled around ancient ruins and modern towns. He knew that Akaba was supplied from, and expected to be attacked from, the sea, so that its front and flanks would be heavily defended, while its rear would be held lightly or not at all. All its guns would bear frontally or to the sides, none would point to the rear. He knew that Turkish soldiers were fanatically brave, but also fanatically rigid; they fought best (as did most troops) when facing the expected; but present them with a surprise, and they would panic. Lawrence had studied warfare over a span of three thousand years, and had learned a very generalisable lesson; if you wish to triumph in battle, and you possess limited resources, attack your enemy unexpectedly. Only thus will you be able to redress the balance of disadvantage against you.

He had all the information he could reasonably hope to glean. What he did not know was either unknowable or else only testable in the event. Such ignorance could only be neutralised by taking risks. And he was a risk-taker.

## Evaluation
Lawrence combined an ice-cold analytic brain with great emotional flow, a most unusual blend. His sheikhs told him that crossing the hundred or more miles of the desert was impossible – sufficient water could not be carried; even camels would die in the midday sun. But Lawrence, though young, realised that men and women will often judge a task impossible if they have never been motivated to do it. They develop a tradition of not attempting it, because they lack the drive to solve the problems posed, or because they fear discomfort or danger.

Lawrence had no intention of travelling across the desert by day. He aimed to go by night, navigating by the stars or by illuminated compass. By day the caravan would dig in for shade at the base of dunes or in ravines. He knew that the journey would be a terrible ordeal, but because he was a masochist and revelled in pain, the prospect of suffering for an enormous reward was delicious, and not to be missed; perhaps it was his prime motivation.

He knew also, because he had seen them in action, that his Arab allies fought best when they were sweeping all before them. Not for them the hard slogging of trench warfare; so he aimed to deliver them in an all-conquering camel charge into the soft rear of Akaba town. He had calculated the risks; they were high. Should they lose their way in the desert, they would all die. If the Turks had fortified the town's rear, or had any warning, he and his sheikhs would be driven off. But not for nothing had a ribald poem written by a fellow officer described him as 'Lawrence, licentiate to do and to dare', and not for nothing was he the illegitimate son of an Irish baronet, whose childhood had been spent under cover in Oxford. So he was entitled to say with Shakespeare's Hotspur, 'God, stand up for bastards', and hope for compensatory good fortune.

### Decision

Taking Akaba from the Turks would be a prize of immense value for the British forces in Egypt. At one stroke it would open up the Red Sea and its hinterland to Allied control. Winning it with a small mobile force and not a large army or a costly naval battle would be doubly worthwhile. So Lawrence had every incentive to be decisive.

He was one of a half-dozen young officers, the rest now forgotten, engaged in guerrilla activities, but only he grasped the implications of the Sinai desert crossing. Testing out this plan before somebody else had wind of it, or he (Lawrence) was replaced in the sector, was clearly a matter of urgency. He had a huge need to prove himself. Small in stature, tiny beside his brothers, unable to call himself by his father's name, forced to live a lie as a schoolboy and undergraduate at Oxford, relatively poor by the standards of other officers, Lawrence's drive for self-assertion was as enormous as it was partly bogus. It would make him decision-hungry, and a relentless sniffer-out of opportunities, and, sometimes, when he seemed to have achieved his aims, it would cause him to repudiate them.

### EXAMINING ALTERNATIVE DECISIONS

There was nothing inevitable about Lawrence's highly considered decision. He did indeed write his own life, as the Sheikh in Robert

Boult's script said, but he could have taken alternative courses of action had circumstances pointed differently.

### Deferred decision
He might, for example, have decided to put off the attack on Akaba. There were rumours that its defenders were starving. Certainly no supplies had reached it in months. However, civilian starvation did not necessarily mean that the Turkish garrison was strapped for food. Troops might still be eating, when townsfolk were dying.

### Impulse decision
He might conceivably have decided to rush the operation with an unplanned dash across the desert. Without detailed preparations, however, the journey would have probably been fatal to all who attempted it.

### Downgraded decision
Altered circumstances might have caused Lawrence to lose interest in the Akaba operation. A point-blank refusal by the sheikhs to help, or strong indications that the Akaba garrison was ready to capitulate, could well have triggered the downgrading. It is a most interesting possibility. There was initially no absolute guarantee, of course, that the Akaba attack would inevitably take on serious significance. Plenty of other targets offered themselves in Jordan, Syria or Iraq, and might have been judged more promising.

## DISTINGUISHING DECISION-MAKING FROM AUTOMATIC ACTS

We need to take the concept of decisional **significance** somewhat further, and clarify the scope of this book as regards the difference between true and automatic decision-making. **Decisions**, like those of Lawrence at Akaba, are **opportunities taken when freedom of action is offered**. Such freedom has to be **perceived**, and it is variations in the ability to glimpse opportunities for decisional freedom that distinguish those who really *choose* from those who, like Sheikh Auda said, *have their choices made for them*.

But, of course, perception is not the sole factor. *There are many situations in life where no choice is open, but a response must be made, so an automatic act or routine operation is the only feasible option.* These are not decisions in either the spirit of this book or in any commonsensical view. They cannot be attached to or understood through our Aims, Information, Evaluation, Decision framework, and no attempt will be made to interpret them thus.

## EXPLORING ALL VARIATIONS

We shall, however, be exploring all possible variations of real decisions. We shall look at the classical, considered, variety (Lawrence's Akaba is our first example). Decisions not to decide, choices made on impulse, acts done in emergencies, or dependent on risk neutralised or accepted, decisions made on ethical grounds, all will be analysed in his book. Each chapter includes exercises to strengthen the skills required. The first exercise follows.

## EXERCISE 1.1

Pick a significant decision that you have made in the recent past. Analyse it (not more than 100 words per component) using the model 'Aims, Information, Evaluation, Decision'. Assess its success (or otherwise) on a 10-point scale, with a score of 10 representing complete success.

# 2
# Focusing on Aims

In Chapter 1 we tackled decision-making from a theoretical standpoint, providing a framework on which the process might be hung. Now we move to practical considerations, and seek to cover that framework with thinking-in-action examples, and also pull from it useful insights. Our framework, Aims, Information, Evaluation and Decision, remains in place, and gives a sequence to this, and following, chapters.

## FOCUSING ON DECISION-MAKING SKILLS

The subtitle of this book is *How to Develop Effective Skills for Making Good Decisions*. Everyday life has now become demanding of skills to an extent never previously approached in human history, and no aspect of decision-making can thus escape the need to be competency-based.

Why do we focus on skills? Because only by breaking down the task into process sub-skills, and practising them as appropriate, can we develop decisional effectiveness.

### Focusing on skills in the Aims element
Whether the context is personal or business we cannot discuss decision-making before addressing its essential first element, Aims. Where aims are lacking, although actions and choices may be seen to occur, such pseudo-decisions in fact lack all the vital components of realistic decision-making: coherence, motivation, focus and, most tellingly in a business context, consent. Inevitably, too, the chances of success for those decisions must be slim.

Aims being so vital, we shall consider the skills that underpin them in detail under the following headings:

- the limbo of aimlessness

- aiming to develop aims

- how aims build motivation
- the organisation and prioritisation of aims
- examining, adjusting and revising aims
- statement of aids and
- aims as a policy-shaping tool.

## THE LIMBO OF AIMLESSNESS

Many years ago I was lamely attempting to explain my confusions to a man of considerable academic achievement who was becoming more irritable by the minute. Finally, being unable to contain himself any longer, he said sharply to me, 'All right, whatever you do, don't drift.'

He was very perceptive. He correctly intuited that I was in a limbo of aimlessness and might only struggle free by action of some kind. Precisely what kind was not important; the vital point was that action, any action, might produce a direction, perhaps even an aim. But drift would generate nothing.

### Developing limbo awareness

It may seem strange to term 'limbo awareness' a skill, but though difficult to practise, and demanded infrequently, it is a skill, even if it is developed to serve one crucial occasion only. It is essentially a skill of recognition, becoming aware, and taking action on that fresh awareness. I was only vaguely aware of my aimlessness and its significance before my mentor firmly indicated it. But from that point onwards my awareness crystallised into an aim-seeking mindset; I knew I lacked the aim and all the advantages that went with it and, furthermore, it showed. I would have been grateful to have been given the 'Limbo aware appraisal' below (Exercise 2.1), if for no other reason than that it would have shown that an attempt to systematise an aim was being made. As it was I had to develop an aim *to develop an aim*, a formidable task of self-generation, which took me a while to master.

### EXERCISE 2.1

### Limbo aware appraisal

Ask yourself the following questions:

- How long is it since I felt any promptings of ambition?

- Did I once have definite aims?

- Has anyone remarked on my evident aimlessness?

- Have I noticed a contrast between my aimless state and the motivated, target-directed attitudes of others?

- Does my aimless state bother me?

- Do I have any insight into my aimlessness?

Then study your answers.

## AIMING TO DEVELOP AIMS

Can the development of aims be an aim in itself? The answer is, yes, if two conditions are met. There must be, first, open acknowledgement of aimlessness, and second, the swift building of a mindset capable of translating needs into objectives. Openly to acknowledge one's aimlessness is not a particularly onerous task; but creating real objectives may prove more difficult. A systematic self-interrogation will probably yield the required insight. Building the consequent mindset will need instructions and exercises.

### Case study: Sam begins to search for aims

It was quite by chance that Sam realised how aimless his life had become. He was sitting drinking with Michael, who was going on and on about how difficult it was achieving his sales targets, when suddenly it dawned on Sam that Michael, despite his gripes, had real objectives to work towards, whereas he, Sam, was like a ship without a chart or compass, steaming nowhere in particular. 'I must do something about this,' Sam thought, 'but what exactly? What do I really need? And where do my true interests lie?'

Although no immediate answers came to him, from that moment Sam was quietly filled with new confidence. He knew that if he persisted with this line of self-enquiry, an aim would eventually emerge.

### Aiming for aims – a combination strategy

When aimlessness has developed into a problem, it can sometimes be solved by combining needs, interests and attitudes into the form of objectives. This approach requires:

- a self-appraisal of needs, and their subsequent ranking by strength and persistence

- a self-appraisal of interests and a similar ranking

- a trial blending of dominant needs and interests to yield a possible structure of aims

- a testing of those aims by comparison with attitudes and values.

## EXERCISE 2.2

### Self-appraisal of needs, interests, attitudes and values

1. Make a list of your principal needs.

2. Refine the list to, say, six items.

3. Prepare a table, and list the needs briefly down the left side.

4. Make a list of your main interests (strengths can be included).

5. Refine the list to, say, nine items.

6. List the items across the top of the table.

7. Cross-reference needs and interests making brief entries, and try to create aims from the cross-reference process.

8. Repeat procedure with attitudes/values.

## HOW AIMS BUILD MOTIVATION

- Motivation, of course, does not completely depend on aims, but they provide a vital, often decisive, input. They make their contributions in two ways, through **formulation** and **reference**.

- In terms of formulations, the act of defining aims causes motivation to shape itself appropriately, giving it clarity and selective strength.

- When reference is in action, continued mental joining-up of aims with motivation helps to reinforce pressure behind decisions and action, giving the latter momentum on every occasion that reference is made.

### Case study: Angela finds encouragement in having clear aims

It took Angela several months to shape her aims for the new charity.

There were so many possible objectives for her. She had to think hard about what was feasible within time and resource limits. But when she finally did have her aims sorted, she quickly realised what a valuable tool for encouragement and self-reinforcement such clarity was. Every time she felt baffled or frustrated, and her resolution was slack, all she needed was to summon up her aims. The act of reference revitalised her. She soon dropped into the habit of regular aim-reviews, particularly at difficult times of the day or during crises. It was something to reach for, and always ready to hand.

## EXERCISE 2.3

### Using aims to build motivation

1.  Develop a set of **self-statements** for aims, for example:
    'This is my aim.'
    'It's been my aim for ... years.'
    'I'm proud of my aim.'
    'I've gone some way towards the fulfilment of my aim.'
    'I'm always ready to review my aim.'
    'I owe it to myself to achieve my aims.'
    Add any other self-statements:

    ............................................................................

    ............................................................................

2.  Identify all motivational needs prompts, e.g. times of low morale, defeatist thinking, etc., and pair such thoughts with the *two* self-statements on each occasion.

3.  Prepare a weekly chart, and note all times during the week when you make these pairings.

## THE ORGANISATION AND PRIORITISATION OF AIMS

We can identify five kinds of aim:

- Overarching
- Immediate
- Unconscious
- Competing
- Re-created.

Rather than defining each in detail, we offer the case study of Gavin (a would-be politician) in a bid to wrap them together intelligibly.

## Case study: Gavin aims for the top

Gavin's **Overarching Aim** is to be Prime Minister. Although he has kept it to himself, this has been his objective since the age of fourteen. Thus far his political achievements have included a ten-year spell as District Councillor, and the Secretaryship of his local constituency party. This **Overarching Aim** keeps him working towards being selected as prospective Parliamentary Candidate at the next election, two years away. But Gavin also has an **Immediate Aim**. He must keep his seat at the forthcoming municipal election, an essential short-term element in his long-term strategy. Gavin may be only vaguely aware, and those close to him may not grasp at all, that he additionally has an **Unconscious Aim**. This is to compete with and outshine his brother, a local business man. This aim has been with him for almost his entire life. It is founded on early sibling rivalry, and probably dates from infanthood.

Gavin, of course, inhabits the real world, where livings must be earned, which means that he has **Competing Aims** of an urgent kind. His position as Buyer in a large, local, supermarket is under threat from rationalisation, and this pressure is aim-competitive in that he has been scheduled for a buyers' training course which conflicts with a vital regional party conference. All of which conflict anticipates the possibility that Gavin will soon have to consider **Re-created Aims** if he is made redundant. A crash course in political research and organisation may offer him the prospect of being an agent or a headquarters worker, key salaried positions on his ladder to ultimate political power, and a useful tactic to simplify his aim complications.

## Coping with conflicting aims

Aim complications of Gavin's size are not everyday challenges. Nevertheless, in individual or organisational situations where aims appear to conflict, or where time-scales appear to conflict, or where time-scales for achievement are variable, some formal effort at organisation and prioritisation could well prove useful.

The **Organisation and Prioritisation Guide** (see box below) is a practical method of self or organisational evaluation. Formal though this method may appear, it should provide a valuable opportunity for skill prompting and practice.

---

### Organisation and Prioritisation Guide

I have **organised** my aims in the following categories:
(*Note aim briefly*)

Overarching.................................................................

Immediate.................................................................

Unconscious.................................................................

Competing.................................................................

I would rank those aims in **priority** terms thus:

1.................................................................

2.................................................................

3.................................................................

4.................................................................

I would assign a time-scale for attainment of those aims, thus:

● within months

● within a span of 1–5 years

● within a span of 5–10 years

● above 10 years

● indefinite

---

## EXAMINING, ADJUSTING AND REVISING AIMS

Aims are not cut into stone as permanent, unchangeable, isolated from reality. Aims are dynamic, flexible, responsive entities, existing to serve, and ready to be made more serviceable.

While to recommend a strict routine might be excessive, there is merit in considering the regular examination, adjustment or revision of aims. We live in a world of flux, where rigidity and over-consistency can seriously damage decisional prospects. What is required, then, is a system for evaluating the status of aims and keeping them in line with current events and needs.

## Case study: Ron switches from playing to teaching

Before the motorcycle accident Ron's aim had been crystal clear, and realisable; everybody said so. But when the knee did not fully recover, despite six months of hugely expensive physiotherapy, paid for by the Club, Ron had to think again. Premier League football demands absolute fitness, and though the knee was nearly right, nearly wasn't enough. Ron was in the first year of a BA degree in Mixed Arts, but when he learned of the Club's decision, he sought out the Dean of the Education Faculty, immediately. 'Are there any places on the BEd Physical Education course?' he asked. 'I've had a change of plan.'

## EXERCISE 2.4

### Examining, adjusting and revising aims

Review the aims you listed in the Organisation and Prioritisation Guide. If circumstances changed, and any of those aims became unattainable, how would you revise your plans?

- My **Overarching aim** is..................................................
  ......................................................................

- My **Immediate aim(s)** are................................................
  ......................................................................

- My **Unconscious aim**, if any, is.........................................
  ......................................................................

If any or all of the above aims became unreachable, my revisions for them would be as follows:

- My **Overarching aim** would become ...................................
  ......................................................................

- My **Immediate aim** would become...................................
  ......................................................................

- My **Unconscious aim**, if any, would become........................
  ......................................................................

## STATEMENT OF AIMS

Whether we wish our aims to be known to others or are resolved to keep them to ourselves, there is no question that they must be stated. The nature of such statements can range from the simple, unvoiced, self-recital of objectives, to the tightly drawn, carefully worded and well-advertised missionary statement issued on behalf of a business concern. In both cases, the purpose of the statement is the same, to spell out to ourselves and others what we aim to do, and to reinforce our intent.

### Case study: Molly aims to cut down on smoking

Molly was a chain-smoker, ordered by her doctor to cut the habit down drastically, or risk emphysema. Her father had died of, or with, that ghastly ailment so she was taking notice by enrolling in the group-practice anti-smoking programme. The practice nurse was the firmest woman she had ever met. She handed Molly a daily reduction chart, double A4 size, with entry spaces for six months. 'Put this on the back of the wardrobe door,' she commanded, 'and fill it in each day of the week. It'll give you something to aim at between the sessions.'

### Using charts

Displays of aims as simple statements are useful, but constructing charts which list target and achievement results, and put the exercise in a time-scheme, are much more motivating and clarifying.

Sometimes (and the psychology of this is still mysterious) the simple act of displaying aims or targets in chart or any other form has an immediate, beneficial effect. In the trade this is known as 'chart-gain', and inexplicable though it mostly is, its benefit in reinforcement terms cannot be underestimated.

## AIMS AS A POLICY-SHAPING TOOL

Aims are not the only tool to hand whereby policy can be shaped, but they certainly figure as one of the most important in any policy-making kit. In organisations decisions are often grounded, hopefully, in policy, and to the extent that policy is shaped by aims, the latter's contribution can have complex and multi-stage inputs.

### Case study: Helen

Helen, who was the Association's Secretary, was forever being pestered by the Board Members over policy. They had an irritating habit of contriving themselves invitations onto local radio (in one case, national television) and then discovering that in interview their understanding of the Association's policy on key issues was uncertain. But Helen was clear enough on policy. She had put out an inventory of members' needs, analysed the returns, and translated them in part into Association aims. That was the policy determinant as far as she was concerned. Aims drove policy, and the bulk of the other activities of the Association.

We can gain an idea of the structure of Helen's aims-driven policy by studying Figure 1. Here is displayed in the left-hand column a list of her aims for the Association, but not complete or put into priority order. Across the top are two specimens of her policy directions; towards the issues of Training and Registration, and Location of Head Office. The chart helps to clarify the links between aims and particular policies. Both aims and policies are sharp and distinctive, and certainly deserve to be understood by any Board member who risks being questioned on them.

| Aims | Policy Directions | | | |
|---|---|---|---|---|
| (Not listed in priority order) | Towards ? | Towards Training and Registration issues | Towards ? | Towards Location of Head Office |
| To double membership in five years | | Not to press for overstringent training or registration requirements | | |
| To create a truly national Association | | | | Seek a Midland location, thus breaking the London bias |
| To... | | | | |

Fig. 1. Examples of aims linked to policy directions.

# 3
# Exploring the Role of Decision-Making in Business Management

Decision-making is a vital managerial skill, but not, of course, the whole management story. Significant decisions in business relate to two specific areas:

- the identification of the size, nature and trends of the particular market the business aims to capture

- the gauging and provision of the organisational means whereby that market can be satisfied.

In this chapter we will focus on four decision-making skills as applied to business markets and products:

1. market research
2. inner sense or intuition
3. standpoint-taking
4. scenarios.

All four are powerful competencies, capable of development on a team or individual basis, and applicable to both small and large businesses.

## MARKET RESEARCH

This is one of the modern foundations of decision-making in marketing. Since the 1950s there has been immense growth in the semi-science of opinion- and attitude-testing, most of it directed at political, social and consumer issues. It is important to grasp that not until comparatively recently, and then by no means universally, did such assessment imply forecasting. In other words, what was tested (often at great expense) was the here-and-now, but not the anticipated, choice. Only in the last decade has research moved into hypotheticals, encouraging subjects into expressing preferences, or otherwise, for as yet unseen products. Such 'suppose' and 'what if' questions are very demanding on the imaginative and projective powers of subjects, and tend to be much less accurate than questions which relate to the here-and-now. People change their minds, or may not know them fully in the first place. Nevertheless, the refinement of such forecasting techniques is the most important task facing the market research movement, the implications of which go to the core of business decision-making.

Whether projective or current in scope, market research is generally organised in two approaches, group or individual, the former associated with panels, focus groups, participant or live-in observation, etc., the latter depending on multiple, individual interviews. Both approaches make much use, not always obviously, of highly structured questionnaires with items tied to preference clusters, and organised with sophisticated mathematics. Both also concentrate mathematically on the representative nature of the samples interviewed, carefully selecting or rejecting responses not considered typical of the consumer world as a whole.

The results served up by market research are always couched in tentative terms, and never delivered 'raw', so that the would-be decision-maker can seldom, if ever, look at the original data of the surveys commissioned. But there is a rule-of-thumb methodology especially adapted to unpicking expert advice of this kind. It goes by the name of Kipling's Serving Men, and may be the great writer's own invention.

## Kipling's Serving Men

Possibly out of desperation at being persistently quizzed as to the origin of his abundant creativity, Kipling explained it away by reference to his 'Serving Men'. He named this staff for six interrogative pronouns, **Who, What, Where, Why, How** and **When** and claimed that answering their self-addressed questions yielded all the material for his novels, short stories and poems. Whether this was, in fact, his creative method is uncertain, but there is no doubting the penetrative power of those questions in opening up a very broad range of obscure operations. Market research is an especially arcane activity, highly technical in some aspects, and dressed up with professional mystique. The Serving Men, put to work, search it thoroughly, as follows:

- **Who?** A two-pronged question, enquiring as to the competence of those who conducted the research, and the degree to which those who formed the research sample were representative of the population as a whole.

- **What?** Addresses the material quality of the research. What was the enquiry content, the question framework, the item structure?

- **Where?** Searches place, the range and area of the research, the rationale for choosing the field coverage, and, most vitally, the degree to which place is generalisable to the market whole.

- **Why?** Asks for the rationale underlying the research method(s) selected.

- **How?** Focuses on these methods and their implementation, e.g. Internet, postal, telephone, focus group, domestic observation, in-depth interview, etc., and seeks reassurance on their respective track-records for this specific research.

- **When?** Has everything to do with the timing of the research, and the possible bearing on the results. **When** is particularly crucial. Events move markets and preferences both decisively and swiftly, rendering data outworn or obsolete.

Supported by the 'Serving Men', decisions about marketing can be made much sharper, and the values of research input thoroughly tested. But in no sense does this ease the decision-maker's responsibility for self-search to great depths.

## INNER SENSE OR INTUITION

Those who totally commit themselves in decisional terms to the expert advice of others, however scientific such advice and the experts who provide it may appear, run risks. This is not a wholly predictable world. Indeed, ultra-modern science suggests it could be fundamentally chaotic and intrinsically impossible to forecast. Statistics may yield pseudo-certainties, but then they are recent formulations. The human mind, however, and especially its unconscious sectors, is not recent; it is as old as time itself, though suppressed in function by modern fashions in forecasting. But men and women also possess their own inner predictive sense, in some cases, as for Joe in the following case study, very sensitive and accurate.

## Case study: Joe sells out before the Crash

In the frenetic summer of 1929, Joe Kennedy, financier, bootlegger and father of a future American president, felt a tingling of unease. The Stock Market had risen uncontrollably, driven up by a booming economy, and the dangerously facile technique of buying-on-the-margin. Warning signals (the reverse-yield index in particular) had been flying since spring, but each time the chartists predicted a downturn, the market rose yet higher. Those who sold in the summer saw their former shares rise and rise, and groaned with anguish. And yet Joe Kennedy, a ruthless, greedy man, was anxious. In October, he suddenly acted. With his portfolio at an all-time peak, he instructed his broker to sell everything he owned. Under protest the broker complied. There followed a fortnight of torment for Joe Kennedy during which he pondered on his sudden, intuitive, decision. But on 24 October he was enormously vindicated: the market broke, ruined the country, and most of the world with it.

Joe Kennedy kept his assets liquid for about a year. Then, sensing that the only growth industry in the USA would be escapist entertainment, he began to invest heavily in films. Not only was this very profitable, it also brought him, as mistresses, several of the most beautiful women in the land.

## What is inner sense?

Joe Kennedy was a far from admirable figure, save for those who find money-making and keeping on a huge scale admirable. But he possessed an amazingly acute inner sense which not only focused on matters financial, but also, since he was a most accomplished womaniser, guided him on sexual forays. What is this inner sense, and can it be cultivated?

Inner sense, or intuition, must depend on the deepest instinct of self-preservation, modified to sensitize the individual to the smallest cues of threat or promise given by others. Several conclusions flow from this definition:

- We can deduce that instinct is particularly useful when ordinary reasoning provides no good guide to action, such as the 1919 Stock Market situation which had become a financial madhouse.

- It is clear that in such a situation, available cues (signs of fear, greed and over alertness) may not be strong, and may need great sensitivity to gauge their trends.

- Confidence is required to act intuitively in these situations, and such confidence can only come from successful intuitive decisions in the past, either situation specific or generalised from other personal experience.

- Intuitive decisions are unlikely to be process-choices (taken as a result of working through Aims, Information, Evaluation and Decision). They more frequently resemble impulse actions – sudden, decisive jumps, impelled by thrusts from within.

## Developing inner sense

Is there any method of **developing** inner sense? The answer would appear to be negative, if for no other reason than the lack of underpinning psychology. But we may be able to **tune into existing intuition**, and maximise available resources, particularly those having relevance to the specific decisional problems we face. One way to do this would be to devise a list of prompt questions for self-appraisal, to ensure that every question had generalisability, and thus make it possible to build confidence for decision-making by accumulating a set of insights into past experience.

## Self-guide to inner sense

1. Are you certain that the decisional situation facing you is one where reasoned judgement is not of significant use?

2. What has been your track-record of past intuitive decisions for this type of situation?

3. Do you have a track-record of past intuitive decisions in any other field?

4. What is your inner voice telling you about this decision?

5. Is there a conflict between your inner voice and the decision that is indicated on limited reasonable grounds?

6. Do others share your intuitions?

7. Can you make a list of all the minimal cues (inner voice prompts) that cluster around this decision?

8. Can you calculate the outcomes of both counter- and pro-intuitive decisions in this situation?

9. Have you encouraged your inner voice over the years?

10. Does this intuition press you hard and feel as if it might convert itself into an impulse to act at any moment?

Consider all ten questions if you are faced by a decision which does not appear to be clear cut and which seems to need more than conscious judgement for action.

## STANDPOINT-TAKING

There are few more important market-research-related skills than standpoint-taking, sometimes termed **allocentricism** ( = 'putting the other at the centre'). Standpoint-taking is the developed and focused capacity to put oneself in another's shoes, view the world from their eyes, and specifically, in market-testing terms, anticipate their preferences. It is both an individual and a group-allied skill, the latter being developed from competencies practised with the former, but more generalised in scope.

Standpoint-taking is as much about the future as the here-and-now, since we seek to share the viewpoints of others not only on current but also on future events. We hope to anticipate their as yet unformed choices and preferences, and thus give shape to *our* decisions on how best to meet their market needs.

Standpoint-taking is a trainable competency. Although individual learning is certainly possible, group instruction is both efficient and, from an organisational point of view, desirable. Two heads are better than one in generating other insights. Moreover, gathering in employee participants for workshops ensures a sharing of responsibility for marketing and builds a common purpose.

### Running a standpoint-taking workshop

Ideally, this workshop requires six participants to give it breadth and leverage while simultaneously keeping it supple. They should have backgrounds and interests to straddle the market target.

*First session*
1. Begin proceedings by setting out the workshop aims, e.g. generally to anticipate the size of the market for the product, and its durability.

2. Continue by giving technical input, e.g. details of product price, availability, putative market, etc.

3. Ask participants to declare their market links, e.g. any special awareness of the target market – residence, children, relatives, friends, visits, experience, memories, etc.

4.  In sequence, ask participants to 'brainstorm' (see Chapter 10) the needs, interests and attitudes of the target group, and the extent to which the product satisfies or aligns itself with these. Record all material produced.

5.  Each participant should then prepare his/her **Ask Around** plan, i.e. a scheme of casual but purposeful enquiry about the product's acceptability, within their own circles and, tactically, outside.

6.  Close this first session, and set a date for the next, allowing ample time for participants' 'Ask Around' to be implemented.

*Second session*
1.  Open the session with a request for participants to report on their respective 'Ask Arounds'.

2.  Discuss material produced.

3.  Provide opportunity for 'meditation'. This is a chance for participants to think themselves into consumer mindsets, preferably with minimum external distraction. Allow ample time both for meditation proper and the vital note-making arising from it.

4.  Discuss meditation notes.

5.  Organise role-play. This will be a buyer/seller role-play with participants alternating roles in an effort to enter the experience of consumers contemplating the product, and retailers selling it. Notes made from these role-plays may reveal much about the product's face-acceptability and/or concealed defects.

6.  Finish by asking each participant to estimate the product's marketability on a scale 1–10, and justify their assessments.

## SCENARIOS

Although learning from the past is a traditional and well-tried method of instruction, there is also a sense in which we can learn from the future. This paradoxical claim is not as strange as it might first seem. The future from which we can learn is, in fact, a projected present, a narrative or a set of narratives of plausible alternative happenings. We call these **scenarious**, a term taken from the film industry which first developed the practice of very detailed script planning so that sequences could be rehearsed and shot in an economic and logical order.

Scenarios, useful for business and personal decision-making, differ from those of the film industry in that they are **speculative**, not scheduled, and also **possible**, not tied to a future planned programme. Speculative though they are, it is useful to identify certain elements which they must possess to function effectively, namely:

- driving factors
- plausible underpinnings
- plots and narratives
- outcomes.

### Driving factors

A driving factor does not necessarily have to be explicit in a scenario, but its force must nevertheless be felt. It implies the circumstances which cause the scenario to be necessary, even vital. Specific business or personal dilemmas, economic or social circumstances or changes can be any or all the needs which bring this method of deciding into being.

### Plausible underpinnings

Again, these do not have to be explicitly stated, but they must be present. The scenario has to be plausible. How likely is it, for instance, that a trade union will press for a higher wage, a dissatisfied customer take his order elsewhere, or a flurry of business activity fall away? The answer lies between 'quite' and 'very likely'; they are reasonable expectations. But plausibility can be seriously challenged by wish-fulfilment fantasies, i.e. unlikely, but desirable, dream events.

I once saw evidence of typical wish-lists intruding themselves into scenarios when I studied a set of alternative outcome scripts of American inspiration, focusing on the future performance of the Norwegian economy. It is no secret that the USA dreads the possibility of dear oil, and consequently looks askance at producer countries like Norway, which take a firm national grip on their resources, excluding globalist interference. Scenarios which depict Norway losing control of its oil reserves, being forced to diversify its economy, and subsequently becoming less prosperous than before, can be viewed as pure and simple wish-lists with no roots in reality.

Their underpinnings are, of course, American economic prosperity, and free-market philosophy, which take no account at all of the self-interest of smaller nations.

## Plots and narratives

Every scenario must tell a necessary and plausible story and, although there is no call for scenario writers to be accomplished novelists or journalists, they must be able to set a scene in words, and push a narrative along. The need for this part-professionalism lies in the operation of the scenario on the imaginations of those who study it. It must engage their interest in order to stimulate their decision-making, problem-solving or creativity, but without material to arouse it, such stimulation is unlikely. There is an old saying, 'Everybody has a story in them somewhere'. We might rephrase this to, 'Everybody is capable of some narrative effort, if encouraged.' It is for the important business task of scenario-writing that such occasional creativity is to be harnessed.

## Outcomes

Scenarios demand conclusions. They are useless if allowed to peter out, and leave no satisfactory ending or summation. The story, driven by business necessity, set in a context of plausibility and narratively engaging, must lead to a conclusion. Only if it has an intelligible outcome will it adequately serve the purposes of a scenario.

The three uses for scenarios are to:

- develop insight into the future

- create new decision-settings

- rework existing decisions.

Thus far we have discussed the scenario as a singular entity but, in practice, if the technique is to fulfil any or all of these three uses, it will have to be deployed plurally at least. This means that alternative scripts will need to be created, generating alternative outcomes.

## Producing a scenario

Realistically, scenario production cannot be other than an irregular activity, and the responsibility of a small, creative, management **team**. But the periodic writing of future scripts with varied outcomes, embodying management aims, must be central to serious decision-making and rated a priority concern. Such a team, though not required to be scripting, must be informally in continuous contact, noting and sharing speculative ideas on future eventualities. The accumulation of such material should govern the rhythms of script production, allowing worthwhile scenario sets to gestate naturally within creative team resources.

The human brain works best by forming **comparisons** – in the case of scenarios, by focusing on the difference between alternative future outcomes. From such a focus, tools to develop insight can be fashioned. The future takes on a notional width, and opportunities, as well as hazards, appear on a mental screen. A system of judging the likelihood of different outcomes is naturally required. This could take the form of a cross-comparison table with entries for the following categories:

- **Logical chain** – covering the links in the chain of reasoning leading to the scenario's conclusion, and focusing on their consistent credibility.

- **Research depth** – gauging the relative depths of research undertaken for each scenario.

- **Centre-taking** – evaluating the plausibility of a scenario by its closeness to a hypothetical centre of possibilities; penalising extremes.

- **Wish-list distance** – assessing the degree to which a scenario conforms to the secret aims of its creator, and consequently lacks objectivity. This category depends on awareness of scenario provenance.

Such a table, completed by independent judges, could be used to test scenario predictions on as close to objectivity basis as feasible, and scores could be given for performance in the four categories.

### EXERCISES 3.1–3.4

3.1 Take *one* of the Kipling 'Serving Men' questions, and thoroughly explore its implications for market research in respect of your product.

3.2 Over a period of, say, six months record every intuitive prediction you have in relation to a future event, and its accuracy in the outcome. If hits or misses can be categories, try to build categories.

3.3 Take any product (not necessarily one with which you are closely associated) and gather up the viewpoints on it of, say, a dozen different persons. Try to anticipate viewpoints before recording.

3.4 Write a scenario, 800 words maximum, under the title, 'The market for our product in 2010'. Arrange for a colleague to write his/her scenario under the same title for comparison.

## UNDERSTANDING THE IMPACT OF ORGANISATIONAL STRUCTURE

One very important factor in business decisions is the shape or structure of the organisation of the business. Whereas even a half-century ago most structures followed a traditional pattern (some version of the military/hierarchical model), in recent years a range of innovations has appeared, often with picturesque names. Among these we focus upon **Silos**, **Shamrocks**, **Stars** and **Currant Cakes**. All these models, and more, can now be glimpsed in organisations small and large. They have been developed in response to global and market pressures, and the transformation of countries into business-driven societies. The important issue for us is the implications for decision-making within them, and what precautions need to be taken to ensure that it is not distorted or frustrated by their particular features.

### Traditional Command and Control Model (TCCM)

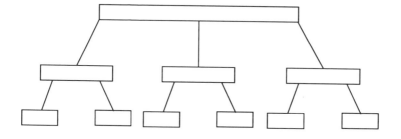

Traditional Command and Control Model organisations have an apparently tight chain of authority and direction systems branching downwards from the top of the structure, with a range of designated and demarcated tasks tied to each level of functional activity.

*Points to note*
1. The many management line connections guarantee a massive bureaucracy, thus indicating great decisional drag.

2. The structure is submarine in system, i.e. relying on the captain (manager) having a clear periscope view. No other decisional input is possible.

3. Middle management do not *take*, they *implement* decisions, and their essential feedback is likely to be reduced.

4. Initiative is likely to be minimal at the base of the pyramid, and 'suggestion-schemes' typically ineffectual.

5. Since consensual decision is disallowed by the structure, all top-down directives must be carried through to the letter.

## The Silo

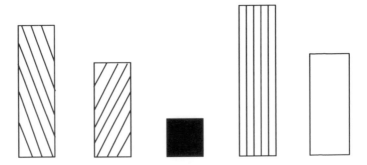

Silo businesses are usually large organisations, divided divisionally and departmentally according to specialities of management and production. Each division, and to a lesser degree the departments within it, has considerable autonomy inside the umbrella company. Silo is popularly asserted to be antediluvian, but it has demonstrated great staying power, probably because national governments, though advocating privatisation, tacitly prefer to deal with its monolithic structures.

*Points to note*
1.  If bureaucracy in TCCM is hampering, the Silo form is stifling, and especially so in terms of inter-Silo communication.

2.  Silos breed isolated thinking, so decisions with inter-Silo significance may be taken without reference to outside impacts.

3.  Silo marketing can be a particularly insular function with other divisions (Silos) excluded from decisions, even though they may have much to contribute.

4.  Global competition can very easily undermine a Silo business since it lacks the flexibility and speed required to adjust to rapid market or cost changes.

5.  In order to function effectively, Silos usually become inter-Silo committee-run, and then evolve into dominant committee structures. Such evolution can be highly inhibiting of swift decisions.

## The Shamrock

Shamrock-type organisations (the terms was invented by Irish-born management academic Charles Handy) consist of three 'leaves' or decentralised elements. These contain key staff, contract personnel and full or part-time workers, often without spatial contact, and linked electronically.

*Points to note*
1.  Intimate contact vanishes in Shamrock, to be replaced by fax, telephone and e-mail connections. Much decisional 'feel' vanishes with it.

2. Contract personnel (even if pre-Shamrock employees) may have risky autonomy through not seeing the full picture possessed by key staff.

3. Savings made on plant and personnel costs by Shamrock can be vitiated in decisional disputes and countermands.

4. Shamrock may well be only suitable for loose, informal, elastic businesses.

5. Despite an image of informal elasticity, Shamrock businesses may survive by means of ruthless, unilateral key-staff decisions.

## The Star

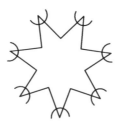

A Star business structure intimately connects an organisation's activities with a small range of large-size customers, with each connection forming a semi-dependent, customer-directed, unit. Large consultancy businesses, especially computer or accountancy in scope, tend to be Star organised.

*Points to note*
1. Large-size customers may have equally large, and sometimes opposed, demands so Star may not be the decisional rest-home commonly supposed.

2. Nor are Star decisions exclusively accountancy-driven; arbitrating between customer-directed Units may bring in other considerations, such as human resources.

3. Three-cornered decisional tensions may be expected – between two customer-directed Units and Star management.

4. Customer secrecy and its enforcement on the Unit may give rise to serious information deficits and, consequently, poor Star management decisions.

5. Stars are vulnerable to tentacle-loss, i.e. buy-ups of Units by customers.

## The Currant Cake

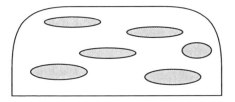

Currant Cake businesses have defined boundaries but inside their organisational space a highly decentralised cluster of currants (operational units) functions semi-independently. Ultra-modern in scope and direction, they have evolved to take advantage of fluid, risky and transient market opportunities, where a single concept seems to answer a current need.

*Points to note*

1. UK experience of Currant Cake is mainly confined to the franchise industry, which is concentrated in the service sector.

2. Decision-making (currants level) is significantly restricted by the terms of franchise agreements.

3. Franchisers do not generally welcome initiatives from franchisees; bottom-up suggestions are discouraged; top-down decisions govern practice.

4. Currant Cake organisations are partly, at least, decision-avoiding and risk-minimising in nature. Franchisers employ few staff; franchisees keep most of their profits.

5. Implicit decision-spreading governs Currant Cake operations. Part-responsibilities are exchanged, and a web of mutual watchfulness is maintained.

## EXERCISE 3.5

### Decisional realities questionnaire

1. Can you place your own business organisation in the range of five models described above?

2. Does it fit precisely, or partly overlap with another model?

3. Does the appropriate 'points to note' list contain items which you recognise?

4. Are there items not present which you would include?

5. **Construct a complete list for yourself including all relevant items**.

6. Does this list completely cover your decisional reality?

7. Do you seek more decision-making autonomy?

8. Is this to compensate for promotional frustration?

9. How much more responsibility are you prepared to accept?

10. **List, in order of importance, the areas in which you seek more decisional space**.

11. Given the model's restrictions, do you consider your decisional prospects in those areas promising or unpromising?

12. What are your possible tactics (assertiveness, negotiation, retraining, etc., for enlarging your decision-making scope?

13. **Briefly describe your tactical programme**.

14. How long are you prepared to persist with your programme?

15. **If you are ultimately frustrated, which alternative model would offer you the best prospect of reaching your decisional goals?**

## EXERCISE 3.6

### Collaborating with a colleague

Arrange to collaborate on this exercise with a colleague in a similar position to yourself as regards decisional space and constraints. **A colleague cannot be a rival**.

1. Separately, complete the Decisional Realities questionnaire in Exercise 3.5

2. Discuss at length entries for items 5, 10, 13 and 15.

3. Revise actions plans on the basis of mutual discussion, letting mutual agreement override initial objectives in every case.

## COMPUTER-SUPPORTED MANAGEMENT DECISIONS

The era of blind-faith commitment to computer domination is gradually fading, but it is worthwhile making a critical appraisal of systems of management support which depend on computer decisions. In fact, no computer ever made a true decision in the entire history of technology. Actions have followed from computer demands, and sometimes led to disasters, but these were never decisions in any real sense. True decisions demand an awareness of circumstances that no computer can or ever will be able to match. Witness the critical part played by the circuit-breaker stock-selling systems in the 1987 Wall Street Stock-Market crash. These ostensibly removed the onus of buying and selling decisions from brokers, but in the 1987 crisis they came within an inch of destroying the market totally, because they were not programmed to recognise the dangers of mass computerised action.

Another example of computerised decisional mayhem occurred in a large company whose stock and order control had been programmed away from human intervention. The fact that stocking and ordering is more an art or knack than a set of calculations and commands was forgotten, until it was alarmingly discovered that the computer had not been asking itself why individual stocks were low or high, or whether they should be replenished in part or full, but had gone on blindly ordering from stockists without regard for company cash-flow or reserves.

Plainly, then, computers do not make decisions. They can help to shape aims, provide information (sometimes too much information), evaluate that information (but they have no value judgement in themselves) and present sets of decisional options. But they cannot *decide* for those who programme them, and if they are allowed to do so, the risks of calamity can be very great.

## Checking on computer domination

As we have seen, computers may have unexpected, unprogrammed and, sometimes, very unwelcome decisional capability. It is certainly worth carrying out a regular audit of all systems where automated options for unsupervised action exist. With this to hand, it is also occasionally useful to simulate such overriding action in selected systems and discover the extent to which human judgement might be sidelined, and the wider consequences if this were to happen.

# 4
# Seeking a Decision-Making Style

What is style in the context of decision-making? We can best define it as:

- a consistent pattern in the way we choose
- maintained over years
- observable in a variety of life-choices and
- part of our fuller personality.

Several possible styles and mixtures occur which can vary greatly in the degree to which they influence choosing. They form a significant factor in personal decision-making and are well worth close scrutiny.

## EXAMINING DECISIONAL STYLES

Broadly, we note four styles or, more accurately, style-combinations. They are not wholly independent, can overlap and can also vary in strength and significance over time.

- **Perceptive/deliberate (P/D)**. A style that would ideally seem to suit a range of decisional demands, yet can have drawbacks if it begins to limit flexibility or creativity.

- **Deferring/procrastinating (D/P)**. Can be driven by calculation or defensiveness, but on both counts may provoke difficulties if overemphasised.

- **Impulsive/indiscriminate (Im/In)**. With its no-thought characteristics and poor judgement combined, only very special circumstances suit this style.

- **Imperceptive/detached (I/D).** A highly egocentric style with limited empathy and reality contact, and almost certain to bring its owner into eventual conflict, if not varied appropriately.

## DEVELOPING INSIGHTS INTO DECISION-MAKING STYLE

There are three reasons why we need to develop insight into decision-making style:

1.  to provide us with wider and deeper self-knowledge, and thus give us greater psychological strength

2.  to enable us to sharpen our decision-making skills in the light of our past decisions and assess the appropriateness, or otherwise, of the styles of choosing we adopt

3.  to give us insight into the styles of other persons, and make us better judges of their possible reactions.

### Self-assessment of style
Study the four guides (A–D below). Each has ten items focusing on the specific, decisional issues of the style. Give each a score out of three, according to the following:

1 – 'I don't see myself as that.'

2 – 'There is some truth in it, as far as I'm concerned.'

3 – 'This is me, no doubt at all.'

Note your individual item scores, and total scores for each guide.

*Interpreting your scores*
Scores on any guide list in excess of 25 indicate style dominance. High style dominance scores should be interpreted with care, and always within an everyday context:

- All things being equal, a high perceptive/deliberate score should not provoke decisional conflicts, unless the stylist's efficiency is reduced by obsessive caution or detail-guaranteeing.

- A high deferring/procrastinating score will fit a decisional context which values caution and considers delay to be an advantage. But outside such a setting, or in a change situation, it will swiftly create a mismatch.

- High impulsive/indiscriminate scores predict mismatch and conflict in almost all decisional settings.

- A similar prospect awaits the imperceptive/detached stylist, but since the style is more evasive than proactive, mismatch will be slow to materialise, although devastating when it does appear.

### Guide A. Perceptive/deliberate (P/D)

1. You approach most decisions with a clear aim in view.

2. You are easily able to discriminate between important and trivial decisions.

3. You can sense when a decision must be taken, even in circumstances where others are unaware of the need.

4. You seem to be able to grasp the essential elements for any decision, i.e. sufficient information, motivation, opportunity, etc.

5. You possess a serviceable routine for taking decisions, which is flexible to different circumstances.

6. You almost never invite another person to make up your mind for you.

7. You seldom choose unless you are sure, and you take great care to make your choices as certain as possible.

8. You do not like to be rushed into decisions.

9. When you cannot decide, genuine doubt is the root cause.

10. You have no emotional hang-ups over decision-making; the process is part of thinking in action as far as you are concerned.

### Guide B. Deferring/procrastinating (D/P)

1. You are only too aware that putting off a decision sometimes means rushed action in the end.

2. You much enjoy either saying or implying 'wait and see'.

3. You take satisfaction in remembering the occasions when changed circumstances made a delayed decision unnecessary.

4. Putting off difficult choices is a well-practised tactic of yours, and is designed to give you time and flexibility for response.

5. Most of your cognitive effort in decisional situations goes into calculating how long you have before you must decide.

6. Deep down you are afraid of decisions.

7. You have sometimes been accused (by others) of dithering or hesitating.

8. Your deepest anxiety is being hurried into a decision by other people.

9. Should the outcome of a decision be a fiasco, you are always able to comfort yourself with the thought that it was rushed.

10. You all too frequently lose sight of any aim when a decision must be made.

## Guide C. Impulsive/indiscriminate (Im/In)

1. Looking back, the reasoning behind some of your decisions seems far from clear.

2. 'No thought' seems to characterise many of your decisions.

3. You are secretly proud of 'not thinking' before you act.

4. You make no real distinction between trivial or serious decisions; they are all nuisances.

5. You enjoy surprising people with the speed with which you make up your mind.

6. You regularly put decisions on 'the back burner' for the thrill of experiencing a rush to delayed action.

7. Looking back at some of your most impulsive and also self-defeating decisions, you would willingly do the same again.

8. Deciding totally on impulse is a great release for you.

9. You can never understand why others delay their choices; the decision is always self-evident.

10. Making a decision without any aim in view can be a thrill for you.

## Guide D. Imperceptive/detached (I/D)

1. When others define their aims you are puzzled at having none of your own.

2. Frequently you are amazed at the degree to which others grasp opportunities.

3. You exist entirely separated from the world of urgency.

4. Other people can never get through to you.

5. You are often surprised when others point out the chances you have missed.

6. Phrases like 'go for it', or 'grasp it with both hands' hold no real meaning for you.

7. Other people often urge you into action, but you generally ignore them.

8. Privately you believe that too much emphasis is placed on decision-making.

9. You are so self-preoccupied that outside happenings pass you by.

10. You have always, since childhood at least, existed for yourself.

## APPLYING STYLE TO REAL-LIFE SITUATIONS

Real-life situations are, of course, the true testing ground for decisional style. It is not so much the isolated happening that may challenge style, but a similar pattern of occurrences or provocations threading through continuous, everyday experiences. Our four typical styles can be projected as mismatching in four sets of circumstances, each very different in its challenge, but similar in continuity.

### Jason – mismatch for a perceptive/deliberate style
Jason had been in insurance, as a marine underwriter, for ten years before a small dispute over performance pay and a refused promotion unsettled him. So on the strength of his Saturday club rugby he went after a Sports Foundation development job. It was a rough selection board; questions came at him from unexpected angles. Sadly, the Foundation turned him down. Jason never saw it, but the board assessor had written, 'This chap is a good, reliable, plodder, but the role needs flair.'

How, precisely, did Jason's style develop its mismatch?

• It was originally not a mismatch, but an adequate fit to the insurance role, which requires a steady, routinised flow of decisions on varying rates.

• But though adequate, the fit could not have been described as superb or seamless. We know this from the performance pay and promotion upsets, and we can speculate that Jason was sometimes a mite too deliberate, possibly even ponderous, so that good underwriting prospects occasionally floated out of his reach.

- Nevertheless the significant, prospective mismatch did not threaten until Jason's somewhat less than perfect performance set him seeking another very different job.

- It seems highly probable that Jason will either go on seeking a fresh but style-matching job, or recognise that he is better off where he is, and make an effort at style adjustment.

## Sabrina – mismatch for a deferring/procrastinating style
'Treat 'em mean, and keep 'em keen' was Sabrina's secret motto when dealing with men, and if you looked like Audrey Hepburn (Sabrina's mother had been a 1950s film fan) this was a reasonable strategy provided it was combined with a sound eventual aim. But if you had no real aim (beyond a desire to keep several men in the air at once) and you failed to notice that time was going by, and you stuck around, then eventually, like Sabrina, you would encounter a terrible truth. The setting being Yorkshire, this truth would be embodied in a very pithy saying, 'She's gone with boots so long that clogs won't look at her.'

Sometimes deferring and procrastinating reflect a personal strategy of seeking advantage. To the extent that Sabrina was devising satisfaction from manipulating and teasing men thus, her style might be said to be tactical if not strategic. But there is more than a flavour here of pursuing a style for style's sake, and such aimlessness does make a mismatch only too likely in the short, if not long run. Time, patience and the needs of others will run counter to this style, and if it does not change, drive it into futility.

## Caroline – mismatch for an impulsive/indiscriminate style
Caroline on the perfumery counter entirely failed to grasp that things had changed when Miss Jones became Floor Supervisor. Miss Jones was straight out of the Company Training Unit, and a tartar. The previous Supervisor had been a blind old bat. Amongst other delinquencies she had failed to observe Caroline trying the lipsticks, holding male customers' hands when spraying perfume on their wrists as samples, raising the skirt hem of the company costume by a good three inches, ripping off till rolls with a jagged

edge, and sundry minor, additional crimes. But Miss Jones had Caroline's number from her first day on the floor, and when Caroline, in a fancy pirouette, knocked over a £35 bottle of Estée Lauder White Linen which shattered on the showcase, she said crisply, 'That's your first warning, Caroline', to which Caroline most impulsively and unwisely replied, 'Get stuffed.'

Tolerant supervisors in large department stores will sometimes overlook the minor delinquencies of pretty, bubbly, careless, impudent assistants if for no other reason than they are good for the showier end of the trade. So, girls like Caroline in the right context will be able to get away with murder for a time. But inevitably the cost-effectiveness of their giddy ways will be scrutinised by new brooms keen to sweep clean. While the context held then, Caroline's decisional style fitted. But woe betide her if she cannot now swiftly adjust it to suit the new regime.

### Roger – mismatch for an imperceptive/detached style

When Roger was thirteen his father began to develop multiple sclerosis of the steadily progressive variety, so that, ten years into the ailment, he had become wheelchair bound. One might have expected that this family crisis would have made Roger more alert to the needs and problems of others, but the reverse was the case. Despite the very evident difficulties that his parents were facing, Roger turned into a young layabout with no regular job, and an infuriating style of treating his home as a hotel. One day, his mother, worn down by years of nursing and penny-pinching and made desperate by his casual, exploitative attitude, said, 'Isn't it about time you found a place of your own, where you could be more independent?' 'Never crossed my mind, Mum,' Roger replied, zapping on a satellite channel, 'Not my bag at all.'

Roger's style and attitude are perhaps best described by the psychoanalytic term 'reaction-formation' – the deliberate opposite of what is expected, and perhaps what he deeply feels. Nevertheless, it is a style which is grossly at variance with circumstances, and bound to be tested ultimately by events. Indeed, parental responsibility and devotion are the main reasons why it has not been challenged before. But this style is now about to become highly mismatching, and if persisted with, must open up a serious family rift.

## VARYING THE STYLES

Those experiencing a decisional style mismatch have two choices, neither easy. They can either vary their style to make a better fit, or seek a fresh setting for the same purpose. The first course is not simple, but is probably more practical than seeking better fits for styles like Im/In or I/D.

Those who set out to vary their style will find the following self-awareness questionnaire of considerable help in developing a style variation programme.

### Self-awareness questionnaire for style adjustment
This questionnaire is intended to provide an overview of decisional style and possible areas of mismatch.

1.   My style scores for the four style lists are:

| P/D | D/P | Im/In | I/D |
| --- | --- | --- | --- |
|  |  |  |  |

2.   My dominant style is................................................

3.   I believe this style has been dominant since (tick):
         childhood
         adolescence
         early adulthood
         adulthood
         middle age

4.   I have been aware of style mismatches in previous stages of my life, specifically in (describe): ....................................
     ..........................................................................
     ..........................................................................
     ..........................................................................

5.   My current awareness of style mismatch derives from:
     (a) a critical incident (describe)

or (b) a long-running friction on events (describe two events)

6. The mismatch is most noticeable in business. . . . . . and/or domestic . . . . . . . and/or social . . . . . . . . . settings. . . . . (give examples).

7. The mismatch centres on (tick as appropriate):
   – tempo problems in taking business decisions
   – missed business opportunities
   – clashes with colleagues
   – rushed decisions
   – empathy failures with partner or relatives
   – social exclusion
   – legal sanctions or disciplinary difficulties

8. I have identified the following items from the style lists as particularly implicated in the mismatch:
   *Items*                      *List*

9. I have studied the Cognitive-Behavioural Psychology appendix, and am taking the appropriate remedial action. (Describe action.)

## Developing a style-variation programme

1. Read the Cognitive-Behavioural Psychology Appendix.

2. Prepare a chart on which to record your continuous daily record of style challenges together with modified responses an their effectiveness.

3. Identify style challenges on the chart by category, e.g. impulse clash, tempo mismatch, observational weakness, opportunity lapse, etc.

4. Using recommended techniques from the Appendix, mount considered responses to every potential challenge; for example coverants for impulse clash; self-cueing for observational weakness.

5. Record via the chart the effectiveness of the various techniques on a week-by-week basis.

6. Vary, substitute or reinforce techniques as and when appropriate.

## EXERCISES 4.1–4.2

4.1 Focus on someone you know well, preferably with a distinctive, decisional style. Choose one of the guides, P/D, D/P, Im/In or I/D, which best fits his/her personality, and complete it on their behalf. Then using the guide items describe in, say, 250 words a matching or mismatching example of your nominee's decisional style in action.

4.2 Imagine you are in a situation in which you face the alternatives of:
(a) varying your decisional style, *or*
(b) seeking a fresh action context where a better fit can be expected.
List the reasons for and against the eventual choice you make.

# 5
# Risk-Taking

## FORECASTING AND ESTIMATING RISK

Every aspect of human behaviour, indeed human existence itself, involves **risk**, which can be defined as **the possible mismatch between intention and achievement, expectation and consequence, or even cause and effect**.

The assessment of risk is vital in conscious decision-making. This chapter looks at **risk-forecasting**, and **contingency planning**, which is the practice of spreading, preparing alternatives to, or generally minimising risk possibilities.

Practising these techniques will, however, never make the decision-making process fully predictable. Human temperament, and especially the great variations between individuals in terms of the meaning of risk, ensures that decision-making is always in the final analysis an art rather than a science.

We shall look at this issue of **subjectivity** in greater detail as we examine the two most important risk processes in decision-making: anticipation frameworks and contingency planning.

- **Anticipation frameworks** are displays of **decisional uncertainties** drawn from past experience, and shaped and organised in such a way as to give limited **guidance** as to what may be expected if a particular decision is taken. They can be simple tables or complex arrays of assembled facts, but they all deal with uncertainties, and all attempt to present risk in forms whereby it can be rationally judged.

- **Contingency planning** entails the exploration of methods of avoiding or minimising risk by various strategies or arrange-ments. **Alternatives, fall-back tactics, insurance** and **indemnity** are typical contingency measures, and may in many instances be the trigger mechanism for a decision by allowing choices to be made which initially bore too great a penalty for consideration.

## ANTICIPATION FRAMEWORKS

The mind is reassured, perhaps even lulled, by structure and when it has some risk framework on which thoughts can be hung, it often makes headway in decisions. There are several kinds of framework and many settings in which they are useful, but the most typical come in tabular, graphic or skeletal form. Some are the products of organised research, others are the result of very informal enquiries. They are never decisive in themselves; many, in fact, require further, subsidiary, frameworks to refine this uncertainty, and all are subordinate to subjective interpretation whether used for business or personal decisions. We begin with a business example.

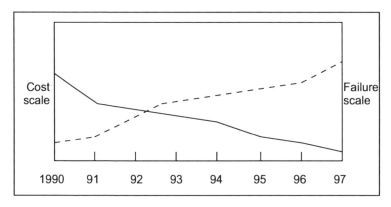

Fig. 2. Unit production costs and component failure.

### Setting production costs against component failure
Figure 2 is a typical cost/benefit graph which a component manufacturer might have drawn up to assist with production costs decisions. It charts two vital variables:

● The continuous line shows unit production costs 1990–1997, a significant and no doubt gratifying fall.

● The dotted line shows component failure within guarantee period during that time, a steady and recently accelerating rise.

There is little doubt that these are causally-related variables, their implication being that cutting production costs (saving on materials and labour) without enhancing or stabilising quality pushes up the component failure rate.

Are they, however, decisive in the choice of alternative actions which the manufacturer faces? We can identify these choices as follows:

(a) A decision not to push the costs any lower, in case the failure rate soars uncontrollably.

(b) A decision to keep trying for reduced costs as long as orders for the components still keep coming.

(c) A decision to raise the quality and precision of the components even if costs are increased.

All three decisions involve risks, and all require more information, possibly in the form of anticipation frameworks, before further choices can be made.

For (a) The manufacturer needs to know how competition is projected for the market, lest stabilised costs make prices uncompetitive.

For (b) The manufacturer must discover the tolerance level of customers for component failure. It may be that lower component prices will make greater failure rates acceptable.

For (c) As with (a), market competition is a key unknown, and the risks it poses must be assessed.

Thus we see that this business anticipation framework begs questions, and despite its power of risk clarification demands further enquiries. The case is similar with personal examples.

| A-level grade | Percentage of finals success |
|:---:|:---:|
| A | 71 |
| B | 19 |
| C | 8 |
| D | 2 |

Fig. 3. Accountancy final examination successes by original A-level results.

## Predicting examination success

Figure 3 is an incomplete expectancy table. At this stage it shows the percentage breakdown by A-level results of first-attempt passes at final accountancy examinations, *but it not based on any actual board or examination.* Let us suppose that a young person with, say, a relevant C in A-levels studies this table with a view to predicting success or failure in the examinations. If the table is an accurate predictor, the prospect is daunting. Only 8 per cent of candidates with C grade A-level results are to be found in the total group. Our young intending accountant is thus required to be a person of overwhelming self-confidence to contemplate adverse odds of this order. The final pass-rate is notoriously difficult; add the apparent A-level handicap and it practically appears impossible. But suppose we have the table completed as in Figure 4 to include the A-level percentage breakdown of those candidates who *failed* the final examination.

| A-level grade | Percentages | |
| :---: | :---: | :---: |
| | Success | Failed |
| A | 71 | 52 |
| B | 19 | 17 |
| C | 8 | 10 |
| D | 2 | 1 |

Fig. 4. Completed expectancy table.

Such additional information will come as a revelation to the intending student of accountancy. At a stroke it subtracts much of the predictive value of A-levels for the final examinations. In purely personal terms it implies that a candidate with A-level grade C is scarcely less likely to pass than one with A-level grade A. In brief, a large proportion of candidates will fail, but their failures will not be significantly predictable from the results of earlier examinations. Other factors are evidently more powerful, and must be identified. What might these be?

In possession of this new information our student might suppose that a decisive factor might well be an enormous amount of hard grind. But hard grind, and the capacity to undertake it, are essentially subjective judgements. If our student, however, believes that his or her C at A-level was paradoxically gained as a result of hard grind, this could decide this issue in favour of trying for accountancy.

### Understanding the value of anticipation frameworks

Summing up this section, we can state that anticipation frameworks are useful servants, but poor masters. They raise more supplementary questions than they answer, but such questions might not be raised without them. They also often plunge their constructors into subjective quandaries which nevertheless may create essential decision-making positions.

### EXERCISE 5.1

### Creating an anticipation framework

Research and present an anticipation framework displaying risk in one of your own future, or past, decisions. This can be in simple tabular, graphic or algorithmic form (see the relevant section of the chapter). It should be capable of a high degree of intimate **involvement**, and a note about the degree of such involvement should be supplied. By involvement we mean the extent to which the specific circumstances of the decision-taker are illustrated within the framework.

## ASSESSING SUBJECTIVE RISK

Even if the risks of different alternative courses of action are clearly displayed, and understood in a precise, quantitative way, there is no guarantee that they will be interpreted similarly from person to person. One important factor in this difference in subjective interpretation is the action of **denial**.

### Understanding denial

Denial is an intriguing psychological mechanism, universal in its operation, Janus-faced, working both positively and negatively in human lives, and very much involved in decisions. Denial protects us from reality, often as much for our own good as harm. Too much reality would overwhelm us; too little might lead us into actions we would regret. When denial comes into play it is reinforced by a secondary mechanism, namely **rationalisation**. This is a reason-providing service, essentially in the business of serving-up plausible and durable reworkings of reality so as to cement us to any action we may have decided upon, and give us a resistance point in case our denial is challenged. There are various forms of denial, some simple, others highly complex. In the following case studies we will focus on four as being most involved in influencing risk assessment.

## CASE STUDIES

### Denial keeps me cycling

I am very aware that nearly a thousand cyclists are killed in Britain every year, and many thousands more injured, yet I regularly cycle to work three days a week. Crash-helmeted, riding on the pavements when cycle-tracks run out, and drawing upon fifty years of expertise (hopefully), I am confident of not being numbered amongst the dead. At the back of my mind, however, is the recollection that, over the last century, two members of my immediate family have been killed and a third severely injured in road-associated accidents. Subjectively, I am ignoring the danger, rationalising it away in a cloud of exercise necessity, economy, environmental care, and macho eagerness to compete with other cyclists. It is a powerful process, this shoving aside of facts. Amongst other events it has withstood the impact of the death of a young motorcyclist on an adjoining road; perhaps I make a distinction between cycling and motorcycling. And each time I complete a successful return journey, I am reinforced in my belief in immortality! I carry on cycling. It is the systematic operation of denial that keeps me cycling in the face of evidence of the specific risk that the practice poses. By way of reinforcement, it serves me up a well-knit set of rationalisations including some plausible contingencies. Thus, I save time, money and pollution, obtain valuable exercise, and, since I wear a crash-helmet, boots and gauntlets, and keep to the cycle-tracks where provided, my precautions are comprehensive and soothing.

But I am denying the range of possibilities, risk and options. These include deliberately avoiding finding out what parts of my route are the riskiest and when; telling myself that the errors of other road-users are unimportant in danger terms; and, most significantly, failing to discover bus times or appropriate routes.

Why am I in this selective denial? In some senses I am fortunate; I have insight into what may be driving me. It is not pleasant to admit that fear of ageing would seem to be the root motivation, but at least I do know that this is a very powerful source, and unlikely to weaken.

A serviceable term to describe my cycling strategy would be **self-relevance denial** (SRD). I do not dispute the accuracy of the cycling accident statistics; *I merely consider they do not apply to me.* It is a common enough form of denial, and it rewards me on every occasion I return safely home.

SRD is all to do with self-relevance, but denial can grotesquely challenge the very *validity* of well-established data, sometimes in ways that cause an observer to doubt the sanity of the challenger, as in the following case study.

### Colin keeps on eating

Colin, who weighed seventeen stone, and rising, pooh-poohed all diet-talk, calorie-counting and exercising. 'How much you eat,' Colin said, 'has no bearing at all on your weight'. His confidence stemmed from a paperback by an American health guru entitled *The Gourmet's Slimming Roadbook* which sang the praises of excess eating, and advocated hypnotherapy as a method of weight reduction. 'I come from a fat family, we're all big people,' Colin would claim. 'Take my mother, she was twice my size, and very quick on her feet.' He did not add that his nimble mother had not been fast enough to avoid a massive stroke, which had killed her at the age of 52. 'All my weight is bone and muscle,' Colin would also often attest. 'If I have any fat on me, it's brown fat; that's not the lethal kind.'

It's all too plain that Colin's denial is in a different dimension from mine. He holds that traditional wisdom concerning the line between overeating and gaining weight is nonsense. This is **counterfactual denial** (CD) and it requires the most powerful psychological motivations to hold it in place. When it appears to 'free' its exponent for a self-destructive decision, one which has a certainty to it, we sense that the sufferer is locked into the deepest of identity crises, and in terrible danger.

CD is a psychological sledgehammer, but there are other ways to deny facts, which exhibit great subtlety and tenacity. Such denial defences are often built with an awareness of where their weaknesses lie, and preserve a careful strategy of never testing them. Take the case of Josh.

### Josh keeps on gambling – and losing

Josh is a compulsive gambler who has belatedly discovered accumulators. This is the practice of placing a sequence of wagers on horses or dogs, with the winnings (if any) being transferred from race to race, the stake consequently increasing and the notional gains also, until the ultimate jackpot of the final race where, if you are very lucky, you make a killing. There is a snag, of course – accumulator breaks are not allowed; you have to bet on a chain of horses, say six from six races. A sequence of two or three wins in a row is not unusual, but hard to extend to six, and you cannot pull out after, say, two. Several times Josh has had the exquisite agony of an accumulator building to £10,000 or more on the fourth race, only to break up on the fifth with the entire stake lost. Josh does not realise that such experiences are very reinforcing, cancelling out the negative impacts of his huge overall losses. He is, however, half-aware of a form of denial which also keeps him at the accumulators. If you add up the odds of an accumulator over six races, or average them, you finish with respectable-seeming odds, say twenty to one, which, in terms of winning thousands for an initial £5 stake, is attractive. But Josh has a strange feeling that if he ever *multiplied* the odds from race to race, he would face final figures that would put even him off betting in this form for good. And yet strangely, in a way he cannot explain, especially since he of all people is always calculating, Josh never multiplies the accumulator odds. It is as if there is a no-go area of his mind which shields such deep longings from reality, and is quite capable of keeping out interference from meddling facts.

With Josh, of course, we again face a very different form of denial. This is a complex defence mechanism which has taken over an established skill in computation and is selectively manipulating it to ensure tight compliance with self-destructive needs. Josh is a virtual master of applied higher mathematics, at least as far as gambling goes. And yet that mastery can be inhibited to serve the compulsive gambler's unique wagering thrills and the lure of great unearned riches. Josh clearly demonstrates **selective denial** (SD).

Thus far we have approached denial from subtle standpoints; our examples have illustrated three methods of thinking about risk, shaped by emotional needs. But there is a form of denial demonstrating no subtlety and very common, namely the tactic of totally forgetting the risk involved in a decision, possibly on more than one occasion. Our term for this is **denial by forgetting**. It can be a persistent mechanism, and the risks run when it operates may be very great, as witness the case of Jacky.

## Jacky

Jacky is a party-girl and her party whirl is a great buzzing blur. It is spun along by a mixture of E tabs and experience-seeking, and more often than not, her early mornings end in a hectic bout of bonking in the rear of some guy's Escort. Jacky can never explain it; perhaps the explanation is obvious, but no matter how long or varied the preliminaries, she never thinks of taking or insisting on precautions. It is not a question of putting it out of her mind; the thought is never there at any time. She could so easily whip into the ladies and work one of the vending machines. She could beg one from another girl. And, most to the point, the final, delicious encounter in the back seat could be on a no-show-no-go basis. But every encounter ends with Jacky's thinking the same thought, 'It just slipped out of my mind.'

### Gaining insight into our own denial
These four types of denial – **self-relevance**, **counterfactual**, **selective**, and **forgetting** – are four common tactics for handling risk predicaments. How can we gain insight into the nature and range of our denials? This is no easy task, but useful steps could include:

- assessing the amount of mental energy we expend explaining away a decision to ourselves.

- noting the instances of others challenging our denials in bold or subtle ways

- realising that our anticipation style has always contained elements of denial

- keeping a record of levels of confidence in our decision-making

- bringing our denial to a counselling relationship.

### EXERCISE 5.2

### Writing a denial case study
Review the various denial tactics as described above:

1.  repudiating the *personal* significance of inconvenient facts – **self-relevance denial**

2.  repudiating the *general* significance of inconvenient facts – **counter-factual denial**

3.  avoiding the exploration of inconvenient facts – **selective denial**

4.    deliberately not remembering inconvenient facts – **denial by forgetting**.

Write a short case study, not more than 200 words, to include one of these denial tactics. Avoid the themes of the chapter studies.

## CONTINGENCY PLANNING

Contingency in practical terms means precaution, and its kernel is the need to guard against the consequences of not having sufficient information about the outcome(s) of a decision. Contingency planning may be essential to such decision-making and may often unlock situations where otherwise no decision seems possible. Such situations arise when heavy penalties may be incurred for a wrong choice and sometimes when all possible alternatives bear penalties for error. In such circumstances contingency planning can, by minimising losses, spread a net under a choice, which although it may not completely salvage the situation entirely, should that choice be wrong, will still enable the dilemma to be broken. Contingency strategists have focused on five main criteria, which should affect any type of contingency planning:

1.    the structure and extent of the unknown information necessitating the contingency plan

2.    the accessibility of the unknown information

3.    the significance of the unknown information

4.    the degree of risk or inconvenience in the non-contingent situation

5.    the degree of risk or inconvenience involved in the contingency plan itself.

   By means of a case study, 'Mr James's holiday', let us tease out the implications of these five criteria.

### Case study: Mr James's holiday
Mr James, who had become progressively more run down in health since the beginning of the year, had determined on a cruise holiday. He was fed up, so he said, with tearing down autobahns and booking into hotels. What he wanted was peace and comfort, and a cruise holiday seemed to be the best way of ensuring this. He read

through sheaves of brochures in search of the right cruise, and finally weeded out two, which took in most of the resorts he wished to visit, and lay within the price range he could pay. Maddeningly neither cruise, however, could be guaranteed. Both depended on delivery of ships. Full refunds of passage monies were, of course, assured in the event of the cruises being cancelled, but no alternative holiday was offered.

This put Mr James in something of a dilemma. He dared not book for both, lest both sailed to schedule, and he therefore lost a substantial booking fee on one as a result. On the other hand, he badly needed a holiday and, if the cruise of his choice were cancelled, he would be left without a break.

The two alternative cruises left on the same day, so Mr James determined to discover a common alternative cruise which needed a very small booking fee, easily sacrificable, if necessary. After a long search he found one. It was not quite the itinerary he would have liked but the final date for payment of the balance of the fare was two days after he would be notified for sure that either of his first choices was sailing or cancelled. To make certain, Mr James was willing to lose his booking fee, and he therefore booked for one of his first alternatives, and this second cruise as well.

It then occurred to him that his holiday might still be jeopardised by illness or jury service, so he took out an insurance policy which guaranteed a complete refund of all holiday expenses, booking fees or passage monies, in the event of his not being able to sail, through whatever cause. And finally he had to face the problem of the restricted holiday schedule of his firm. There was absolutely no doubt that if he missed his summer break through illness, he would not get another fortnight in July or August. However, he was a senior employee with four weeks' annual leave, and apart from the summer months the holiday roster was flexible in advance. He therefore blocked himself a second holiday period for the end of September, knowing that if anything went wrong with his first fortnight he could take another break then. If all went well he would be able to unblock this period, and take it at Christmas. And to make things trebly sure, he found a September cruise which was virtually 'walk on' and for which only one month's prior booking was required.

It was fortunate that Mr James went to all this trouble. A fortnight before he was due to sail, he received notice that he was required for jury service on the sailing day. It was a case of fraud, involving a quarter of a million pounds, and it tied up judge, counsel and jury for a month. Mr James paid his first-choice booking-fee loss out of the insurances he collected, stood the second cruise loss himself, swiftly reserved himself a passage on the September cruise, and took his holiday with relief.

## Applying the five criteria to Mr James's case

*1. The structure and extent of the unknown information*
Mr James had two dubious areas (which to a greater or lesser degree affected other persons) – the ship delivery and the jury service. The first of these was a hugely complicated entity, involving the possibility of labour disputes, component deliveries, weather conditions, management muddles – an immense structure, in fact, of interlocking uncertainty. Jury service was a different matter, a random selection of householders, organised by local officials into a kind of lottery, but one which could not be avoided, at least not by Mr James. However, Mr James knew sufficient about these areas of ignorance to satisfy the first of the criteria.

*2. The accessibility of the unknown information*
This was another issue altogether. The dubious areas were almost completely inaccessible for different reasons. The dockyards were many miles away (one was in Bremen) and even if Mr James had set himself the task of telephoning dockyard managers (he did not know them) the information he would get would not necessarily help him. In fact, there were just too many people to telephone. As to the selection of juries, this was a guarded, bureaucratic secret. Nobody could be told which householders from which area of the city were being put into 'the hat' for drawing out, and thus the unknown in this case was completely inaccessible. Short of bribing officials at the City Hall, or conducting a shipyard survey (both enterprises fraught with difficulty and risk), the information was inaccessible.

*3. The significance of the unknown information*
Mr James was under no illusions about the significance of the unknowns: they were vital. No ship, under the terms of the passage contract, meant no holiday. And jury service, being inescapable, meant no holiday either.

*4. The degree of risk or inconvenience and the acceptance of risk in the non-contingent situation*
The risks on both counts were considerable, and Mr James was not prepared to accept them. There had been a run of cancelled sailings

(not to mention some disastrous trips) when ships had not been ready on time. As to the jury commitment, Mr James had lived in the city over fifteen years without being called, and he realised that if the ballot were run on a diminishing number of ballotees, his name was about to be chosen. There were risk in another direction too. He'd had a threatened heart attack the previous year, and plenty of medical warnings about relaxing. The job he had was particularly exacting, and the prospects of a second attack were considerable. In personality Mr James was a man who liked matters 'cut and dried'; if there was anything that upset him it was uncertainty. He was not a risk-taker. Such chances as he had taken in his life had been surrounded by much anxiety, and he'd therefore been conditioned not so much by ill luck as by the stresses of risk-taking.

*5. The degree of risk or inconvenience involved in the contingency plan itself*

As Mr James contingently planned it there was little risk or inconvenience caused. He was prepared for the cost of insurance, and the loss of a second booking fee. These were small prices to pay for a cast-iron guarantee of a certain cruise. Setting this outlay against the possible loss of salary which an illness might cause, Mr James considered that he had a bargain, in terms of both relaxation and peace of mind.

## Going for economy

Contingency, as we have shown, means having reserve plans worked out in case a choice turns out adversely. But contingency plans should not be a synonym for elaboration; they should be an exercise in economy, lest the whole purpose of the contingency be negated, *the safety net becoming more elaborate, beautiful, precarious and attention-demanding than the acrobat.*

If we examine 'Mr James's holiday' in a systems manner we shall see that the way he structured his contingency plan involved economies through common safety nets.

He had two alternatives, exclusive as it happened, but he was able to cover both with one contingency item. Whichever he chose, had it let him down, he could go back to his common contingency items and still have his holiday. He also linked the insurance and the holiday switch plan to the alternative first choice. In fact, what he did can be shown in a simple algorithm (see Figure 5).

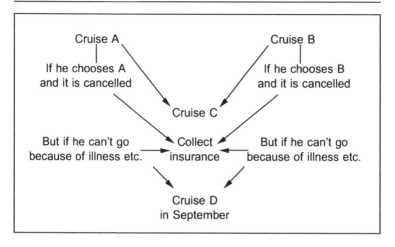

Fig. 5. Mr James's contingency plans.

This is an economical plan. All contingencies are covered, and mostly interconnected. Little or nothing is left hanging, the whole contingency situation is bolted together tightly.

## Limiting the contingency structure

Of course, Mr James could have been far more elaborate in his contingency planning. He could have insured himself against the possibly of being made redundant before settling the balance of the fares, and therefore of not being able to go at all. He could (possibly) have insured himself against rain or bad weather on the cruise. However, he did not do this, and put a limit to the contingency structure he built. For one thing, all these precautions would have cost more money; for another, they would have taken up too much time; and for a third, he would have been covering eventualities that were either very remote, or not (in the case of dying) worth specific insurance.

In fact, Mr James only lost his deposit on Cruise C (he obtained a full coverage from the insurance company for his Cruise A loss). This, plus the insurance premium, was a small charge in the circumstances, and in Mr James's view entirely bearable. He had balanced out the advantages of this degree of contingency against the disadvantages and costs of a more elaborate contingency scheme. It did, in fact, work out satisfactorily for him. Bad luck struck him; the decision he took was risk-laden, but disaster was converted into moderate inconvenience.

Juggling about with holiday dates and holiday choices (where there is some choice) gives an excellent opportunity for contingency planning. This is not the general rule, however. In many decisional situations there is no possibility of building up any contingency plan, the risk cannot be quantified in terms of monetary loss, or the feasibility of alternatives is questionable.

## EXERCISE 5.3

Select and describe very briefly one of your own decisions for which a significant amount of contingency planning was necessary. Then take the five necessary criteria of an optimum plan, as listed above, and identify how those might have featured in your decision.

# 6
# Gathering and Processing Information

We have already identified and partially tackled the first of the four key decision-making components, namely **Aims**. In this chapter the focus will be on the second and third components, **Information** and **Evaluation**. From a broad perspective, we shall be examining the role and range of Information, the various tasks of gathering it, judging the amount needed, and the depths to explore it. Then we shall shift to its Evaluation, the many formal and informal techniques by which its significance can be judged, including schematic, numerate analysis, decision-tabling, intuitive processing, values and moral considerations with their weightings. We shall thread several case studies, some long-running, others brief and limited in scope, through the chapter material, and refer to them in advance, currently and retrospectively. Before this phase, however, it could be useful to look at decision-making as part of a wider world of problem-solving.

## PROBLEM-SOLVING AND DECISION-MAKING

For a fresh decisional perspective, problem-solving technique provides a way of opening up our ideas to new insights. There are all manner of styles of setting decisions within problems, but the framework below is a very simple, useful structure.

| FRAMEWORK | |
|---|---|
| **Problem types** | **Solution methods** |
| Decisional | Displays |
| Procedural | Reorderings |
| Solutional | Modellings |
| Generative | Searchings |

Within this framework we can locate any human problem, whether of thought or feelings, and match it to any solution. As a general claim this is entirely warranted, but particular applications may cause difficulty. Let's break the framework down:

'Decisional'    means    'issues to be separated and compared'

'Procedural'    means    'priority to be established'

'Solutional'    means    'precise answers to be found'

'Generative'    means    'material to be developed'

Now, with a little additional detail, we can see how the problem types form.

- **Decisional** – sets a range which includes anything from a pilot's decision to abandon a take-off, to a person's choice between several attractive lovers.

- **Procedural** – comprises all problems which demand an order, or a rearrangement, for a solution, e.g. how to teach a child the time, or the Court Clerk's task of managing the legal hearing of a case.

- **Solutional** – demands precise answers, or accurate tools, e.g. the designer of equipment, or the debater in Parliament.

- **Generative** – has to do with creating new forms, materials, data, devices. Everything from poetry to fashion is encompassed.

Now let us shift our attention to the solution categories.

'Displays'      means    'internal/external comparisons'

'Reorderings'   means    'varying and prioritising items'

'Modellings'    means    'seeking and developing useful analogies'

'Searchings'    means    'sifting available material for ideas/idea-combinations'

How do these categories expand?

- **Displays** – comprises the widest possible range of choice systems from the job-seeker's analysis of the merits/demerits of several possible posts, to the airline pilot's swift appraisal of his instruments before take-off is attempted.

- **Reorderings** – deals with any form of fresh item-sequence. For example, which composition should start a concert, or the priority tasks for a sales campaign.

- **Modellings** – focuses on every form of solution-finding which employs analogy-thinking, e.g. wind-tunnels for aircraft design, role-playing for psychotherapy.

- **Searchings** – implies any method of teasing out relevant ideas from unexplored sources, e.g. a mother's quest for party suggestions or a writer's pursuit of 'local colour'.

In the framework we note that **decisional** problems have **displays** as their most appropriate solutions. Parts of this chapter will show just how useful such displays of sourced information can be when choices must be made. **However, a problem as a whole can be much more than the key decisions within it, and solving it can bring in methods other than Displays**.

We shall see shortly in a case study just how a couple, faced with a complete change of lifestyle as their *total* problem, not only needed to make a key purchase decision for which they used both **searchings** and **displays**, but had to go further. That key purchase decision committed them to **reorderings** and **modellings** as solutions to their total problem, and without such supplementary techniques their lifestyle change plan could not have been fully implemented.

Thus the framework's clear significance can be seen; within it a **decision**:

- may depend on one or more solutions, but when taken (solved)...

- may introduce other non-decisional, but important, problems to be solved.

## SOURCING INFORMATION

As already emphasised, sourcing information is a core task in decision-making. The following four questions in various ways probe the process, and go a considerable distance towards making it explicit.

1.   How much do we already know?

2.   How do we set about seeking more?

3.   How do we test the validity of what we discover?

4.   To whom do we go to gain expert advice?

## LISTING WHAT WE ALREADY KNOW

It's not difficult, though it may require methodical listing or note-taking, to summarise everything we know about a given decisional topic. The real challenge comes, though, when we ask ourselves whether we know enough. When is enough, enough? There is no easy answer to that question; it is highly contextual and individual. But there are some rule-of-thumb guides to be explained.

Listing what we know is a task of method. Let's take the personal history of Peter and Anne to demonstrate.

### Case study: Peter and Anne explore a change of lifestyle

Peter is 43, married with two children, a teacher wanting to leave teaching. He has just received a substantial legacy, and he and his wife, Anne, also a teacher, hanker after running a village post office in the West Country. With this general and urgent aim, the pair of them settle down to record everything they know about post offices and the West Country. Fortunately, they have a word-processor!

It isn't long before they have built up a mass of preliminary information, a real hotch-potch, childhood and adult, holiday memories, film and television episodes, books and articles, West Country people they have known, gossip, folk-lore, food; if it can be recalled, they write it down. Soon, five thousand words have accumulated, and then, totally drained, they set to organising the material into categories. It is at this point that the size of their research task becomes clear; it emerges as soon as they find that they are short of material to put into some very important additional categories, namely:

- a range of sub post offices for sale in the West Country
- information on mixed retail prospects in areas they may wish to explore
- county development plans for the local economy
- population statistics and age pyramids
- specialist accounting and retailing.

Another four or five categories occur to them, one by one, as they begin their sourcing and sifting of information. There is also the deeper consideration of the information they as a family bring to the later assessment and evaluation task; for example, their personal values, individual needs and prejudices, unconscious attitudes and motives. As teachers they are both used to teasing-out information and summarising it for instruction. Now they are engaged on the task of instructing themselves. There is no shortage of sources.

## SEEKING MORE INFORMATION

Sources of information include:

- **asking around** – relatives, friends, acquaintances
- **written material** – books, newspapers, magazines
- **broadcast sources** – TV, radio, Internet
- **targeted research** – libraries, resource centres, official publications
- **market research** – surveys, questionnaires, focus groups
- **consultancy access** – expert opinion, project planning.

All such sources can be networked and cross-referenced. It is via such processes that $2 + 2$ in informational terms may come to equal not 4 but possibly 5. But the material that is derived must be understood, and judged reliable if it is to be decisionally useful.

## UNDERSTANDING THE INFORMATION

Before we can use information in a decision, we need to understand it. There are no easy routes to understanding; the path can be very rough, and made more difficult by the problem of determining the extent to which we **need** to understand, as much as whether we understand **sufficiently**.

One useful method is the **fragmentation** routine, which is a simple technique of breaking down a task into its possible constituent parts.

### Understanding fragmentation
First, we have to tackle the task of breaking the problem down into sections. Even the most intact-appearing problem is decomposable

in the end. Often a good way to **decompose** a problem is to:

- write it out again in different words, *or*
- put it into diagram form, *or*
- express it mathematically.

One of these ways is almost bound to show up systems, or connections, and once it does, then the problem is decomposable. When a problem is decomposed, it does not matter how many pieces there are. All that matters is the existence of a set of sub-units to the whole.

We then look through the pieces calmly and pick out those which:

- we have met before in some manner, *or*
- feel more confident about than others.

These are the pieces to tackle first. We need not fret about the actual relationships of these pieces. They can be central or marginal to the main problem. The only thing that matters is that we have found one or more 'fragments' that we can start on, since even to start is an advance. The reasons why we attempt to break problems down are:

1. The brain is a comparison-seeking computer and, if even the smallest **analogy** is suggested to it, it may rake around and find others.

2. We develop **confidence** which, though nobody understands its nature in mental terms, is very important in intellectual success. We have to make the most of every scrap we can gather up and if we have even the smallest legacy of confidence from the past to help us with a present problem, this may give us the necessary 'lift off' to solve it.

### Solving the pieces

Now we have to try very hard to solve the piece we have chosen as a starter. As soon as it is solved, it must be displayed together with its links to other places.

We have to ask ourselves if there is anything in our solution of this first part that can help us with the remaining parts. And we tell ourselves that there is one piece already solved, or completed.

## Unblocking the blockages

Suppose we are faced with a **blockage**. In this case, we can try the decomposition strategy again, but this time not on the problem as a whole but on one of the pieces that still resist solution.

Will one of these break down? If so, we have probably separated out a very small problem indeed, the solution of which may not affect the total problem very much, but may still enable us to say: 'There is one more little piece solved. Now, what remains to be done?'

## TESTING RELIABILITY AND VALIDITY

Having gained sufficient understanding, how then do we test the reliability or validity of our information?

## The validity checklist

1. **Is it consistent internally?** Does it hang together logically? Are there contradictions? Matters affirmed at the start, denied at the finish, or vice versa? Statistics faulty? Tables not adding up? Percentages awry?

2. **Is it objective?** Does it take a detached view? Or is it a piece of propaganda? Did somebody write it who had a special interest in writing it a certain way?

3. **Is it too brief?** Is it too short for real sense? Is there just not enough of it to make it meaningful?

4. **Do I understand it totally?** Have a real grasp of it? Sufficient to explain it to somebody else?

5. **Do I understand it sufficiently?** Have I just enough to use it? Some parts are too difficult but these are not significant, or so I believe.

6. **Is it in context?** Does it form part of a whole? Is it one of a series? Is it part of a book? Is there something before, or after, to give me confidence?

7. **Is it complete?** Is it properly finished off? Do I sense omissions? Significant gaps? Somebody has edited it overzealously?

8. **Does it come from a prestige source?** Is the writer well respected? Well known? At the head of his/her field?

9. **Does it come from an expert source?** Is the writer an expert? Has he/she any relevant qualifications?

10. **Is it focused?** Does it seem to be directed to me or somebody else? What is the target? What is the audience?

This checklist of questions can be applied to any piece of information, and provide a **validity scale** on which to place it. **Peter and Anne** have assigned a possible score out of seven for each of its items, and use the totals as a check on all their researched material.

But items (8) and (9), **prestige** and **expertise**, are of particular concern to them, dependent as they are on specialist information from agencies and associations concerned, for instance, with:

- the management of sub post offices

- the policy of the Post Office in respect of sub post offices

- the essentials of small retailing

- the business of a newsagency

- village development, local authority organised, and several other, highly relevant, sources of expert advice.

## ASSESSING EXPERT ADVICE

There are two components to expert advice, the **advice itself** and the **reputation of the expert** who provides it. In practice, the two are very closely combined, and the structure that follows brings them together.

The **AMPFLER** structure is so called from the initial letters of the seven criteria summarised:

A stands for **Accessibility**, the degree to which the expertise is conveniently available. It also includes the important aspect of the expert's nearness to other experts, a significant factor in potentiating expertise.

M stands for **Manipulability**, the amount that can be extracted from the expert. Manipulability varies, but it is hard-headed to seek out the maximum amount possible.

P stands for **Personal appeal**, the degree of rapport between expert and client. This is far more important than ever realised; the effectiveness and assimilation of the advice to a significant extent depends on good personal relationships.

**F**  stands for **Fee**, the field of sliding scales and consultancy charges. If the fee relationship is felt to be just, then the advice will not be blocked or distorted by resentment.

**L**  stands for **Level of expertise** offered, which must be matched to the need as precisely as can be judged. Over-egging is as futile as under-egging in mixing advice and requirements.

**E**  stands for **Expert qualifications**, e.g. the accreditation, memberships and experience possessed by the expert, and judged to be appropriate to the advice sought.

**R**  stands for **Recommendation**. All things being equal, a recommended expert is preferable, if only because of the reassurance that recommendation provides. But recommendation may need to be tested for its own sake.

**Peter and Anne** bring in the AMPFLER structure whenever they are confronted with information from an expert source and need a handle on it. They also supplement AMPFLER with the validity checklist to give themselves a sharper focus. They understand the limitations of these aids, realising that beginners are always in the hands of experts, but are at the same time confident that as mature people they can sense a hollowness at the heart of a bogus or unsupported statement. They also possess developed male and female intuition, the general role of which we have already explored in Chapter 3.

## MORALS AND VALUES IN DECISION-MAKING

In this section the emphasis is on moral considerations and value judgements in coming to decisions. But we need not expect much enlightenment on either issue from Peter or Anne. Neither is in the least respect morally challenged by the vital decision they are undertaking, though there are some values that they hope to uphold or strengthen by it.

Any **moral commitment** they had to teaching twenty years ago has been entirely destroyed by what they perceive as a deliberate government campaign to downgrade the status of the profession, subjugate it to employer and parent power, and turn over its management and inspection to reactionaries and the tabloid papers. In addition, Anne has been demoted in the department she herself started. So quitting teaching seems good and right in every sense.

However, their decision will need to incorporate important **value systems**, for instance:

- ensuring that their daughters' educational prospects do not suffer
- seeking a community which will be congenial, where they can mix easily
- balancing the advantages of village life with the possible disadvantages of lack of amenities, etc.

It will be these and other values, quantified or otherwise, that will be crucial in how they select material and evaluate it for their final choice, as we shall see subsequently.

Meantime, let us examine a decisional dilemma with a very strong moral focus.

### Case study: Bridget gives Rob a second chance

Bridget is senior personnel officer of a large firm of clothiers, and her moral dilemma is whether or not to sack Rob, her assistant personnel officer. Despite her joggings, he has not completed the performance assessments. He deploys all manner of excuses: the section heads have been obstructive; the test agents have sent the wrong protocols; he's had the flu; the Union kicked up a fuss over some of the early gradings, etc. You name it, Rob has encountered it. So, the assessments aren't ready. So, she will face a deal of flak from Accounts when they demand the figures. So it would be very satisfying to exculpate herself, partly by telling the Finance Committee she's let Rob go. So, so, so. It is very tempting, and yet she hesitates. The morality of the decision bothers her. She resolves to lay out its various aspects in a rough, branch framework, built up on questions. The first question is:

*Is it right for me?*
This is not an easy question to answer. Certainly ridding herself of Rob might make her life easier; he's always been an anxiety. On the other hand she picked him, and everybody knows it. There is the problem too of dismissal warnings. Has she carried out the procedure correctly? Probably not, if Rob were to go to the industrial tribunal there is no knowing what the result might be.

*Is it right for Rob?*
It is his first post, and being dismissed might put an end to his career

in personnel. He's also moved in with a partner, and Bridget has learned that the young woman is pregnant. Is Rob owed a chance?

*Is it right for the other employees?*
In a strict sense it is not right to keep Rob. In theory the other employees stand to lose bonuses, but in practice Bridget knows that the bonuses, if any, will be backdated, and that she will figuratively stand over Rob to see that the assessments are done. As regards Rob's other activities, it has to be admitted that he provides an acceptable male face to Personnel, the workforce is 80 per cent women.

*Is it right for the firm?*
Of course, it is not right for the firm to carry an ineffectual employee. At the same time, Bridget has a responsibility to try to make Rob more effectual, and to limit any real damage he might do, until either the opportunity to move him on comes up, or his performance improves. In addition, the firm's attitude to personnel management can hardly be described as enlightened, and Bridget therefore does not rate its moral interests as high as she might have done in other circumstances.

In the upshot Bridget decides to give Rob another chance. She has to admit to herself that the morality of this decision is important. It could almost be called decisive, because the balance of alternatives without it is so evenly poised.

## USING THE INFORMATION

### Peter and Anne display the results of their research
Figure 6 is Peter and Anne's decision table. It's a simple display in appearance, but a substantial amount of research work and enquiry have gone into its construction. At the top we have four possible post offices in four villages, two in Devon and one each in Somerset and Cornwall. These four comprise a short list from a hundred properties considered, and around a dozen actually viewed. Much background economic investigation has been put into the localities of the four villages, focused in part on the long-term business potential of their respective post offices, all of which have additional retail premises attached. It is this work that informs the **potential** factor in the bottom left-hand column, and enables Peter and Anne to assign varying scores, in this case out of 15, to the four cells on this rung of the display.

| Compared for | Somerset PO. A | Devon PO. B | Devon PO. C | Cornwall PO. D |
|---|---|---|---|---|
| **Appeal** out of 10 | Pretty village on the Levels outside Bridgwater 7 | Caravan village, near Barnstaple, very breezy 6 | Posh hamlet up river from Dartmouth 6 | Drab, desolate tin village near Camborne 3 |
| **Cost** out of 5 | Very reasonable; has changed hands twice in 10 years 4 | Reasonable, present owner retiring on health grounds! 4 | Top of the range, all manner of improvements, very hopeful! 1 | Give-away; Post Office and shop closed for 19 months 5 |
| **Potential** out of 15 | Some doubt about farming; too much 'set-aside'. Also Supermarket quite close 8 | Summer, lively; winter, dead. Farming seems steady plus a little light industry 10 | Fast becoming a retirement hole; will the Navy leave? 9 | Subject to Euro-development decision; may be substantially grant aided 7 |
| **Score** | 19 | 20 | 16 | 15 |

Fig. 6. Peter and Anne's decision table.

The factor above is **cost**, i.e. the actual cost of purchasing the shop-cum-post-office. Peter and Anne are not strapped for money; they have the legacy, and their mortgage is 90 per cent cleared, so assessments on the cost rung are out of 5, which represents the factor's scale of importance, and gives an appropriate adjustment.

**Appeal**, the top factor, is more important. Peter and Anne, together with their family, consider it vital to feel at home in the village. Such a feeling is, of course, rooted in a compound of social acceptance, environmental and amenities. This last is of considerable significance; Peter and Anne have two daughters at secondary school, faced with the taxing problems of changing schools. Transport issues loom large in family calculations, and influence the assessments across the ranges.

This is an economical decision table. It contains only three factors and four options, and delivers a narrow preference for the north Devon village. Clearly, the table could include more options, though it might become unwieldy. Other factors might be necessary in other circumstances. Suppose, for example, that Peter or Anne need to visit elderly parents. Then access to the main West County line would become important, and could more sharply differentiate a village's offerings.

Nevertheless, as it stands the table is a powerful instrument for decision, and could well be the trigger for Peter and Anne's choice in its own right. But it would not, of course, solve the wider problem of their family move and change of direction. If we refer back to the **framework** (see page 80) it is clear that before they are fully settled, they will need to draw upon other solutional elements, for example:

- **reordering**, which will be required to set up the smooth sequence of selling up, buying and moving

- **modelling**, which will be the process whereby they transform themselves from teachers to counter-clerks and shopkeepers and assume new roles.

Nevertheless, in framework terms the dominant element in their problem is the **decision**, and they make their choice by **researching, selecting and presenting material for a display**.

### Using more complex decision tables
Peter and Anne's table seems a simple presentation, although it contains and refines an enormous amount of information, allowing

them to introduce a range of different practical and value judgements. There are, however, situations, often business ones, where such wide considerations are not decisionally important, and the need is to pack the table with as much quantifiable information as it can hold. Let's take the case of a small manufacturer faced with a decision on whether to re-equip his factory with new machines to produce a new product. Core component information is as follows:

- The low estimated sales of the product are 100,000 units a year.

- A suggestion has been made to produce that number, but no more, by rebuilding old machines.

- New machines might be bought with a capacity to produce 150,000 units per year, and more.

- There are possibilities of sales in excess of 100,000 units.

Faced with this span of core components the manufacturer draws up a table (see Figure 7). Down the left-hand column, he sets the

|   | Possible unit sales | 1 25p Convert old machines Max. cap. 100,000 | 2 50p Buy new machines Max. cap. 250,000 | 3 35p Do both |
|---|---|---|---|---|
| A | 100,000 @ £1 | **Likely profit £75,000** | **Likely profit £50,000** | **Likely profit £65,000** |
| B | 150,000 @ £1 | NO GO | £75,000 | £97,500 |
| C | 200,000 @ £1 | NO GO | £100,000 | £130,000 |
| D | 250,000 @ £1 | NO GO | £125,000 | £162,500 |

Fig. 7. Manufacturer's decision table.

possible unit sales. Across the top he puts the three alternatives:

1. Convert all the old machines, in which case the unit cost will be 25p.

2. Buy new machines, in which case the unit costs will rise to 50p.

3. Do both; that is, convert the old machines to a capacity of 100,000 units, and buy sufficient new machines to produce up to 250,000 units if necessary.

Then he calculates his possible profits. Of course, when he surveys the table more factors emerge, but these are not strictly of the numerical kind. He has to estimate, for example, the likelihood of the various unit sales. After discussion he learns that A is very likely a 100 per cent certainty: B, 75 per cent; C, 25 per cent; and D, 10 per cent. He tries to bet on near-certainties and therefore discards C and D from his display. After thinking carefully, he decides on No. 3. (do both). This way he covers himself against several eventualities. If the firm sells 100,000 units (A) he makes an average profit; if its luck is in and it sells 150,000 units (B), he makes a better than average one. In any case, he does not work himself out on a limb, and expose himself to the likely low profits of 2 (buy new).

## EXERCISES 6.1–6.6

### 6.1. Key components and core tasks
Imagine a decisional situation in which either a key component is omitted, or a core task is left undone. Outline the possible outcome of such a decision when taken.

### 6. 2. Problem-solving and decision-making
Refer to the problem-solving framework (page 69). Recall one of your significant problem-solving successes, and identify its components in the eight-cell frame. Describe the solution sequence.

### 6.3. Sourcing information
Imagine you have an important decision to make. Prepare a list of potential sources of vital information.

### 6.4. Validity testing
Refer to the validity checklist (page 75). Score every item on a scale of 1–7, 7 being the highest validity. Then select three sample pieces

of information (newspaper reports, etc.) and score them using the checklist.

## 6.5. Moral decisions

Examine the morality of any significant decision taken by you during the last decade. To what degree was it a morally justified decision? For you, for others, as a whole? Set out your respective justifications.

## 6.6. Preparing decision tables

Imagine you are deciding to move house. Prepare a decision table which includes four properties, and compares each on three weighted criteria. Use Peter and Anne's table as a model.

## Making the Decision

### ANALYSING THE COMPLEXITIES OF MINDSET

It is essential to understand the very complicated mental activity that takes place at the moment of any decision. **Mindset** describes that crucial mental state when the combination of **mood, need** and **knowledge** crystallises into decisive action. It is a powerful but essentially neutral state. Within it all kinds of decisions can be worked, be they considered, impulsive or deferred; the mind is set to do what it wants to do because all the necessary conditions are present. A theatrical analogy is useful here. If mindset is stage and scenery, mood, needs and knowledge act out the decisional drama on it, and conclude it to their script. But without mindset, there can be no play.

### UNDERSTANDING MOOD

Mood is realm of feeling and can vary both in nature and intensity, though it is commonly experienced as familiar and intimate, keeping to a level tone. Mood in decisional mindset may be apprehensive, confident, depressive, excited, bored or detached, but can also show none of these features, being indistinguishable in feeling from everyday experience. Mood becomes significant in decisions precisely when it presents as apprehension, confidence, depression, excitement, boredom or detachment.

The **apprehensive** decision-maker will tend to hesitate as will the **depressive**, fearing the worst outcome. Those **excited** or **confident**, whose aims and needs are in decisional harmony, will press forward with their choices. **Boredom** and **detachment**, however, introduce an unpredictable factor; whim and external pressures become powerful influences on such states and can transform them, paradoxically, into impulsive action.

## UNDERSTANDING NEEDS

Needs are emotional pressures that reveal themselves in thoughts and actions expressive of their release or resolution. They are experienced as wishes, drives or pressures from within, but are also influenced by external happenings which arouse, strengthen or weaken them.

### Changing needs

Needs can fluctuate in their intensity, and change considerably. They may do this over time as a consequence of maturation and experience, and also in response to pressures from outside the self. For example:

- The slimming need of a young woman of 20, locked into a competitive desire to be attractive and perceiving it to be essential, may have weakened to nothing as she arrives at 40, married with a family, and feeling no drive to compete whatsoever.

- A man of 50 who perceives himself comfortably off, with no immediate or desperate need for money, may find that the threat of redundancy and pension-gap or inadequacy transforms his previous nonchalance into a great drive to acquire money at all costs.

This second example is particularly instructive. It demonstrates that needs can change swiftly, being awakened, strengthened or weakened by events.

### Knowing the different needs

The mix of needs, with their varying and sometimes cancelling pressures, are vital to an understanding of decision-making. There appear to be ten of them; some almost, but not quite, overlapping; others rare in operation, but worth detailed analysis, and all capable of the most astonishing variations in motivational influence as prompted by circumstances. This section focuses on needs analysis and the essential contribution that needs make to delaying, aborting or triggering a decision.

*1. Need for an aim*

'I wish I knew what I was really after.'

Having an aim, and even more important, a clear one, is a

significant need in itself, and one which, when satisfied, can act as a trigger for a decision. Just as important, as will shortly be explained, is the requirement for **aim** and **need** to be in harmony, since conflict can bring disaster.

## 2. *Need for security*

'I don't want to be left worse off as a result.'

The cultural/political thrust to make life more insecure has raised this need's significance considerably. Caution, careful risk-estimation plus an unwillingness to lose face are its fundamental characteristics. It can operate variously, e.g. as a blockage on decision if security is threatened thereby, or as an incentive to decide if a securer objective can be gained.

## 3. *Need for correct mindset*

'Before I make a decision, I need to feel absolutely right in my mind about it.'

Mindset is very difficult to describe, and the need to establish it is best termed a desire for completeness and thoroughness. If it is possible to satisfy this need to feel that everything necessary for consideration has been considered, then the decision-maker is reassured about outcomes. Whatever the outcome, the mindset being right relieves the decision-maker of guilt and self-recrimination.

## 4. *Need for more information*

'I just don't have enough to go on.'

This need is past experience crying for help, well aware that it is risky to choose on the basis of insufficient material, but that there is more available, if it can be gathered up. It is essentially a risk-driven need and can only be satisfied when the perception of risk is reduced by appropriate accumulation.

## 5. *Need for reward*

'I want to see what's in it for me before deciding.'

Need for reward is often driven by past decisions which have yielded dubious or unrewarding outcomes. The need therefore is not only for gain in itself, but also for the reinforcing experience of reward which may make the decisional process easier in future.

### 6. Need for action

'I never waste much time dithering; just make up your mind, that's all you have to do.'

This need is close to (8) below, but shows the more positive aspect of decision for decision's sake. Nevertheless there is a compulsion to shorten time for judgement which can be risk-laden, especially if this need is the sole motivation.

### 7. Need for delay

'The longer this takes the better, as far as I'm concerned.'

Need for delay can be associated with memories of negative outcomes from decisions, with consequent reluctance to take risks. But it can also take a decisional style form as calculated deferral, or decision-not-to-decide, as covered in Chapter 8.

### 8. Need for relief

'I'll be glad to get this over and done with.'

This need may sometimes be associated with 'decisionitis' or decision for decision's sake, a condition to be examined later in the chapter. But it can also be aroused, and strengthened by external pressures to decide, imposed by other persons and escapable only by deciding in their favour.

### 9. Need for a sponsor

'I'm looking for somebody to make up my mind for me.'

This need often springs from a deep lack of decisional self-confidence, based on adverse, past outcomes. But when it is expressed openly, as in the above phrase, it is usually a tactical concession to group pressure, and does not imply that the spokesperson is handing over total decisional responsibility.

### 10. Need for closure

'I can't wait to get this all wrapped up.'

This is a subtle but powerful need, very much cognitively driven, and concerned with outcomes; in particular their completeness, meaning or justification. Need for closure reflects anxieties about uncertainty, and has compulsive and obsessive features especially in connection with order and neatness.

## Highlighting the key needs

Five of the above list of needs have particular significance for decision-making:

- need for **security**
- need for **reward**
- need for **action**
- need for **relief**
- need for **closure**.

They can drive from within or be prompted by pressures from without. They can operate singly or in combination, but however deployed in action they usually shift the needs-balance strongly away from hesitation and towards decision.

Up to this point we have analysed key and subordinate needs as if we were always fully aware of their power and presence in our conscious minds. But consciousness is not the only significant domain for decisional mindset. There is another area, not as obviously experienced, but none the less important.

## Understanding the unconscious mind in needs analysis

Beyond doubt, the unconscious mind has a decision-making role, but before we identify it, and more usually show how it fits into the process, we must understand what the term 'unconscious' means.

**Unconscious** in this context does *not* mean asleep, though some unconscious decision-processing *can* be carried out during sleep. A closer synonym is **unaware**; we are not consciously in control of the thought process, yet it is continuing without our supervision. We need to grasp that conscious thought is not capable of covering the vast amount of possible thinking that our minds can generate; its focus of awareness is limited. Yet much is going on elsewhere, and it is this semi-independent mental work which can have some powerful products, emerging as

- **intuition**, a sense of certainty without justifiable evidence
- **motivation**, a fresh or renewed urge to action
- **conclusion**, a solution, supplied indirectly, to a problem consciously posed.

These products, often crucial to choice-making, are blends of **cognitive** (ideas/comparisons) and **emotive** (feelings/instincts) thinking. The unconscious mind, with encouragement, is often very effective at delivering these products. Although its direct connections with the outside world are limited, and it has to depend on the conscious mind's perceptions for much of its factual input, it has two advantages:

- first, and most telling, is its unlimited **access to memories**, the individual's essential databank

- and, second, almost as significant, is its **privacy**, the state of being left alone to work by itself.

This **independence** makes managing the unconscious mind challenging but rewarding. All three products can be encouraged to greater or lesser extents, but their management depends on delicate techniques of recognition and reinforcement.

There is a range of possible ways of gaining **access** to true views or feelings. They all involve exploiting opportunities when levels of conscious awareness or control are lowered, and the unconscious makes itself known. Such opportunities occur in:

- twilight states, or waking to sleeping, sleeping to waking episodes

- dreams of all types, including daydreams and reveries

- recurrent fantasies, usually of the waking variety.

*Twilight states*
We shall explore the usefulness of twilight states for solving problems in the Appendix, but there the focus is on their role in determining clear motivation. Feelings are not as clearly identifiable as solutions or creations in such states, but they can be explored by means of self-posed questioning. A range of possible enquiry forms is available, for example:

- What are my real feelings about this decision?
  Provide me with a word that describes my real feelings?

- Which of the following words describes my feelings?
  I will supply some words.......................................

- Am I masking my true feelings?
  Supply me with a situation in which my true feelings can emerge.

*Dreams and daydreams*

By no means all night dreams can be recalled, but those that are recallable, and deal with decisional problems (only a small minority), may provide intriguing insights into unconscious attitudes. Although some claim to be able to manipulate dream-states, this is a very specialised ability, and most dreamers will be left only with their dream on waking. Nevertheless, the feelings of a dream are important, especially so if they happen to conflict with conscious attitudes. The phenomenon known as **dream-left-over**, when dream feelings are carried over into the following day, is also significant. If this time does not harmonise with conscious waking attitudes, then a would-be decision-maker would do well to consider very carefully the advisability of going ahead with a decision apparently made.

*Personal example*

I recently decided on a fresh method of advertising one of my consultancies, entailing considerable planning and expense. I had virtually committed myself to the project, when I had a dream in which I found myself full of criticism and doubts, most of which focused upon the project costs and vital energy expenditure. So persistent was the dream tone the following day that I postponed the whole advertising plan for the immediate future, deferring a decision until I felt more optimistic about it. Nothing has subsequently happened to make me regret my deferred decision, so it is very possible I was suppressing my doubts very forcibly, so forcibly that my unconscious mind could find no way other than a dream to warn me of facts I was denying. Looking again at the needs list (page 86), I can see that a pattern of needs denial was revealed to me in my dream. In detail, I had not acknowledged a need for delay to myself; I also needed more information, and my need for closure could more accurately be interpreted as a drive for security.

## REVISITING AIMS AND ASPIRATIONS

### Aims and needs

In previous sections we looked at **aims** and ways to refine and arrange them in some detail. Now we tackle the equally important task of ensuring that they reflect real **needs** and are a realistic expression of them. Aims and needs do not necessarily live in harmony. Sometimes aims are formulated and pursued without much regard for real needs; especially if it is not easy to identify and describe the reality of the latter. But it is vital that aims and needs are well orchestrated in any decisive action. If they are in significant conflict, the results can be calamitous, as witness the story of Alan.

## Case study: Alan opts to fly low

Because he felt ambition was expected of him, Alan let his name go forward for the 'fast-track' trainees scheme, a programme of accelerated promotion that his firm was keen to launch. There were rewards aplenty for successful young managers: prestige, high salaries, a company car and leisure perks. The firm was putting most of its eggs into this incubator scheme in the hope of winning a competitive edge in an increasingly difficult market. Alan was not particularly introspective, and thus did not realise that his decision to pursue this aim held implications that challenged some of his deepest needs. He took security, stability and certainty for granted (provided by his living at home with his parents, near to the factory, with relatives in the vicinity, etc.) and never envisaged himself being uprooted.

So, he was totally shaken when the Training Officer said in passing, 'I expect you'll settle down all right in Runcorn.' 'Runcorn!' Alan said, 'that's near Liverpool.' 'Correct,' said the Training Officer. 'You didn't expect to stop here on the Scheme, did you? That's part of the point, widening the trainee's horizons.' Alan could have replied that he did not now fancy having his horizons widened, least of all in Runcorn, but instead he simply said, 'I'm sorry Mr Lewis, I don't want to go on with the Scheme.'

For several reasons, notably that the firm took a jaundiced view of potential high-flyers deliberately flying low, that decision did Alan no good at all.

Imitative though this aim of Alan's most certainly was, he would not have come to grief had he also mounted a strong need for reward or, possibly, for action. But the risk from borrowing aims which do not match needs is always great and those who run it can expect events to challenge them at any time.

## Harmonising aims and needs

Before deciding an issue of importance it is always wise to ask yourself several connected questions:

1.  Do I have a good grasp of my aims?

2.  Do I know what and how much I want?

3. Do I really own my aims?

4. Are there other owners?

5. Do I know my needs?

6. Is there a possibility of a clash between wants and needs?

7. Will this clash be manageable?

8. Which will take precedence if it is not manageable – wants or needs?

## BALANCING NEEDS IN DECISION-MAKING

What makes us finally decide? The truthful answer is that we do not know. But we can theorise that a kind of imbalance of needs must exist within the mind whereby action and non-action are poised in such a way that while both remain unequally loaded, choice is suspended. This is a simple model of what is certainly a far from simple situation, but our plan is to show the model at various stages of imbalance through the next and subsequent case studies.

### Case study: Daniel dreads moving house

Daniel is under pressure to move house. His wife, Christine, is applying it, laying it on with subtlety, as women are wont to do. She points out that they are 'empty-nesters' and not big entertainers, so that four bedrooms, once so necessary and so very convenient are far more than they require. She points out that though their house is new, it is not as new as it was, and will soon want some very expensive repairs. There is also the question that young as they feel, they are getting old, and the garden is large and its plants are lusty. So, they should be looking around, she says.

But Daniel, like most men under pressure, is saying nothing. What painful anti-moving memories does Daniel nourish? One is a distant childhood recollection of a chaotic, wintertime, family move, arriving in a strange, freezing, empty Victorian mansion, and feeling absolutely desolate. Then there is a memory of coming home in his twenties to his parents' next purchased house, finding his father struggling to lay a carpet, and a month after that, his father's sudden death. More recently, he remembers with a shudder, was their own bungled move to this present house; a small van arriving when a large van had been specifically ordered, with the whole move having to be spread over two days and two deliveries. He has recollections too of being gazumped in particularly awkward circumstances, of discovering that nothing would fit, and perhaps most irritating of all, of needing to get rid of a gang of repossession agents two months after moving in, the previous owners having left owing extended credit debts everywhere. So, all in all, when contemplating a move, Daniel's mindset is *not* filled with a pleasantly itchy adventurous glow; his mood most closely approximates to a gnawing dread.

On the other hand, he is bound to concede that over the twenty-five years they have lived in this present house, there have been changes for the worse. Concorde flies over twice daily, climbing-out and splitting the heavens with thunder. In the interests of preserving more genteel areas, the District Council has allowed a supermarket to open nearby which has quadrupled the traffic, and generated an irritating amount of parking outside his house. Neighbours, very different from those he recalls in times past, have moved in, and are making their presence felt. They have statement Alsatians or Retrievers, and leave them to roam in their gardens while at work. These poor, lonely dogs yap continuously, but the District Council, which has a 'hands off' philosophy, will not issue orders to restrain them. Surreptitious businesses are being run in the vicinity; not quiet concerns, but band-saw-thrumming enterprises, beginning early, finishing late, and working weekends. An Italian style of behaviour seems to be the social norm; car horns are blown on arrival, departure, recognition and frustration. Barbecues smoke every summer Saturday and Sunday, their aromas persisting for hours. But despite these manifold irritations, Daniel cannot decide, and so he says nothing.

His needs balance can be set out as in Figure 8. Although his need for relief from decisional pressure is a key need, it is outweighed by two minor and one key need.

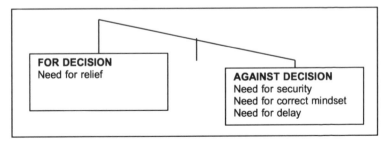

**FOR DECISION**
Need for relief

**AGAINST DECISION**
Need for security
Need for correct mindset
Need for delay

Fig. 8. A needs imbalance for Daniel.

## Unexpected changes

But this situation of imbalance, not altogether unpleasing in its indeterminacy, cannot endure indefinitely. Daniel is to be jerked suddenly out of its soothing state by big changes to his lifestyle. One afternoon he is summoned to the Managing Director's office and told that early retirement has been decreed for him, and ten other senior employees. The terms are not generous; pension blunders and corporate take-overs have cut monthly payments drastically, and expected lump sums have been halved. He is left to bridge the gap from his present age 55 to the time he can draw his retirement pension. His wife, two years his junior, has the same time to wait also.

With little prospect of earning anything of significance, Daniel has to come to a decision. His need is for financial security, and this can only be provided by generating some investment income. There is only one way to do this: sell their large house, move into an economical flat, and invest the balance obtained. Daniel does not wait for Christine to suggest it; he heads for the estate agents immediately.

So now let's redraw the needs imbalance to reflect Daniel's fresh circumstances and new need pattern (see Figure 9). Altered circumstances have brought two more key needs to alter the original imbalance, and need for security has transferred itself.

Daniel has come to a decision, but if, like him, you are in a serious dilemma over deciding, it is useful to have a method of reviewing needs systematically. The needs checklist below provides a nine-point summary of all that a decision-maker requires to mount a systematic review.

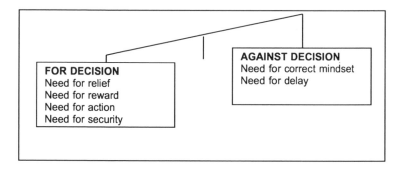

Fig. 9. A new needs imbalance for Daniel.

## Needs checklist

1. I realise that to know my needs completely is not possible; nevertheless, I will try to gain as broad a view as I can.

2. I know that over time needs change, but I do not expect my current needs to lose their strength abruptly.

3. I will pay attention to my daydreams, night dreams, fantasies and reveries for clues as to my real needs.

4. I will examine my everyday patterns of preferred behaviour to guide me in detecting and assessing my needs.

5. I will pay attention to others when they identify my need patterns.

6. I will occasionally list my needs, and describe them in simple terms.

7. I will arrange my needs in order of strength.

8. I will occasionally audit my needs to see to what extent they have been met.

9. I will always strive to keep my needs and aims in harmony.

## Abnormal needs

Two needs on the needs list – need for relief and need for action – can transform decision-making into a **compulsion**, if their drives get out of hand. In the following section we shall examine varieties of this compulsion, and show how devastating its impact can be on organisations or individuals when self-control has been lost.

## AVOIDING 'DECISION FOR DECISION'S SAKE' (DECISIONITIS)

There are two forms of **decisionitis**. The first and by far the most common is the 'no-thought' type, characterised by a compulsion *not* to consider the implications of any significant choice on its merits, but to bring the frustration of being asked to choose to the swiftest possible end by an act of decision.

The second, rarer, type takes the form of a compulsion to seek out opportunities for decision often in the least appropriate circumstances and make choices more in a spirit of bravado than necessity. They take, in reality, passive and active forms, the passive being characterised by fatalistic avoidance of responsibility for exercising personal choice, while the active is opportunistic, never letting judgement interfere with the delicious satisfaction that decision-making generates.

### Case study: Mark (passive decisionitis, need for relief)

Everybody said Mark was irresponsible and that was the truth. He did not like making choices, even the smallest conflict irked him, and he usually rushed all decisions, or wheedled somebody else into making up his mind for him. It wasn't that he was stupid; he just did not want or could not bear to settle down and think anything through. It was almost as if the process was painful for him, and the urge to put it behind him irresistible.

One day, however, a really important decision came up: he had to decide between a range of differing life insurance options, each providing a set of benefits which needed to be carefully considered. Mark's broker was a highly responsible person. He emphasised the necessity for Mark to develop a future script, a view of his possible circumstances over a span of time, and to judge the differing sets of benefits accordingly.

But the broker's well-intentioned efforts had a totally paradoxical effect on Mark. He recognised at once a familiar demand on him for a considered decision, but it was his secret boast that he had never considered any matter deeply in all his life. It was almost as if he had been commanded to be hasty and superficial in his judgement, possibly responding to some deep-seated need to punish himself.

So, in the upshot he scarcely glanced at the policy options, and plumped for the one that had the shortest amount of text. It was twenty years before he realised that he had the wrong policy.

### Case study: Patrick (active decisionitis, need for action)

Patrick had been on one of those decision-a-minute courses where the training consists of a series of in-basket exercises supposedly simulating the role of actual management. But to blame the course for his ailment would have been to confuse cause and effect. Courses of such kind drew in people like Patrick, already seriously infected. He was bad enough before he went. Margaret remembered his first day in the department. She had set out four branch memoranda with notes as to their progress. 'No need for any action yet on any of these,' she said. 'In fact, the longer we hang fire on Schedules 23A and 36C the better. There's still a load of question-marks over them.'

When she got back after an interminable session with the Adjusters, Patrick greeted her with the smile of a satisfied infant, hands finally on a rusk. 'I've signed the lot,' he said, grinning complacently.

### Tackling passive 'decisionitis'

In a very real sense this book seeks specifically to help those suffering from passive decisionitis. If on completing Questionnaire A below, you find you have answered all or all but one of the questions in the affirmative, you should study the Cognitive-Behavioural Psychology Appendix (pages 153–159) with great care. Cognitive/Behavioural Psychology offers a feasible method of combating the denials and blockages of decisionitis, and should be absorbed accordingly.

### Tackling active 'decisionitis'

Realistically, we must recognise that many, possibly all, sufferers from active decisionitis feel reinforced and comfortable with their ailment, and may be unaware or unconcerned by the occasional havoc it wreaks. Questionnaire B, then, is best completed by an observer, who will have to make allowances for the intimate nature of the last two questions, but who may regard a score of 6 or more affirmatives as a cue for action. What this action might be is beyond our scope to suggest. We can only state that people with markedly active decisionitis can wreak havoc in settings where deliberation and judgement are vital.

### Decisionitis Questionnaire A

1.  Do you feel under pressure as soon as the need for a decision appears?

2.  Have you always shied away from decision-making?

3.  Is your usual reaction to a demand to decide to avoid the issue as long as possible?

4.  When you are obliged to choose, do you rush the process?

5.  When you have rushed the process, do you experience a feeling of relief?

6.  Is this feeling of relief coloured by apprehension or doubt?

7.  Are you happiest in a setting where indecision is the norm?

### Decisionitis Questionnaire B

1.  Do you actively seek out opportunities to take decisions?

2. Does the indecisiveness of others act as a challenge to you?

3. Do you pride yourself on the speed of your decisions?

4. Does the slow tempo of others irritate you?

5. Can you often glimpse the need for a decision when others see nothing?

6. Are you pleasurably aroused by the thought of deciding an issue?

7. Does taking a significant decision give you a deeply satisfying afterglow?

## EVALUATING DECISIONAL PRESSURES

Readers who have come this distance can be forgiven for supposing that all the work of decision-making is individually organised, and that pressures on how, what and when to choose come from personal sources inside or outside the self.

This is not the whole story by any means. Individuals are not mental islands with absolute sovereignty; they form part of a huge social network and via its connections they are intimately influenced in all their active thinking. The word 'influence' barely described the social process looked at from the standpoint of our original decision-making model:

- The individual's **aims** are in part shaped by social objectives.

- **Information** for decisions is often gathered as, when and how the outside world dictates.

- The **evaluation** of such information is governed in part by society's norms, values and techniques.

- The act of **decision** itself, which appears so much under the control of the individual judgement, whim or mood, is significantly influenced by pressures from without.

It is this last function of the model that is most vulnerable, and we shall concentrate on it appropriately.

### Case study: Sophie hesitates over the contracts

Sophie had only been Commodity Director for three months, but already it felt like three years, sometimes thirty. Her promotion had been very sudden; out of Standards, where she'd been Eric's deputy, and into Commodities over the head of Thomas who had taken her coming very ill. His reaction had been to press her to pass the six contracts that her predecessor, Alec, had been stalling over, before his coronary. 'Press' was somewhat of an understatement; bully, harrass and dog her might have better described it. 'If we arrive at this merger' (he was referring to their imminent take-over by JTP) 'without these finished,' he said, covering her desk with spread-sheets, 'we shall be up shit-creek.' Of course, as Sophie knew, and dithering Alec had known before her, this choice was not as clear-cut as Thomas was making out. There were other contractors, not JTP-associated it was true, but steady, reliable folk. And some intuition, an indwelling, half-painful doubt, made Sophie hesitate.

Thomas was in a state of suppressed rage and disgust with her. One afternoon she heard him on a crossed internal line say, 'Don't talk to me about decisions; what she needs is a bomb under her arse to make up her mind for her.'

The next morning Sophie came in early, full of vicarious resolve. She had decided to pass the six that morning. When she looked into Thomas's office he was glued to the *Financial Times*. Wordlessly, he showed her the headline: 'JTP merger-bid collapses. Shares tumble £130 million).

'What a bit of luck,' Sophie said.

### Analysing pressures

Being put under decisional pressure is a severe challenge for anyone, and without a scheme for analysing such pressures, one's chances of negotiating the situation satisfactorily are slim. The decisional pressures audit below provides an instrument, and reference should be made to the Cognitive-Behavioural Appendix for psychological guidance.

### Decisional pressures audit

*For completion when under decisional pressure*

1. Pressure is being exerted on me to reshape my aims on this issue.

2. The information I need for a decision is being withheld/ selected/researched/slanted by others.

3. I am being required to evaluate such information against a social, economic, moral or scientific frame of reference other than my own.

4.  My timetable for decision-making is being altered to suit the convenience of someone else.

5.  This decisional pressure is being applied from a source superior/of equivalent status/inferior to me.

6.  I am ready to bow to this pressure.

7.  I shall not be bowing to this pressure unless circumstances change considerably.

8.  I am in deep conflict over this pressure.

9.  I see the need for unified policy decisions and understand the necessity for pressure to produce these.

## EXERCISES 7.1–7.4

### 7.1. Understanding the terms

| **Mindset** | **Mood** | **Need** |
|-------------|----------|----------|
| Framework | Tone | Drive |

Add *two* more synonyms to each of the above terms. An example is given. Use a Thesaurus if necessary.

### 7.2. Exploring the unconscious

Keep a monthly diary, and record day and night dreams, half-waking fantasies and reveries, together with other evidence, to provide you with a comprehensive view of your needs, consciously and unconsciously expressed.

### 7.3. Understanding key needs

Write a short (200-word) case study in which the pressure of a *key* need brings about a decision.

### 7.4 Making compromises

Compromise can be a useful tactic for reaching a decision when external pressure is balanced against internal needs. Imagine such a decisional situation, and devise a compromise solution which allows the decision to be taken.

# 8
# Deciding Not to Decide

## REASONS FOR NOT DECIDING

What fundamental reasons may underline a decision not to decide? In order of importance these could be because:

1. we are in no fit psychological or physical state to make decisions (**danger time**)

2. we lack some decisional information or action which we consider vital to choosing (**insufficiency**)

3. we simply cannot decide between various options; they seem equally attractive or repulsive (**parity problem**)

4. we are unsure of the outcome of a decision, but sense that delay may be to our advantage (**options open**).

Although all four may appear generically similar, in operational terms there is a distinction between them. The first signifies **self-preservation**; we are avoiding a decision because we fear that we are in no fit state to decide. Numbers 2, 3 and 4 are, however, broadly **tactical**; we calculate rightly or wrongly that it may be **profitable** for us to defer our choices.

All four, however, can accurately be described as **positive** stances. Paradoxically, this means that although faced by various uncertainties (ambiguity, doubt, anxiety) creating caution, the decision-maker is still positive, recognising that eventual choices may have to be made, and ready to make them at some future time. This positive quality even attaches to 'danger time' deferral, which we shall tackle first.

The technical term **contra-indication** is frequently employed in what follows. It simply means that the state of illness is of itself a warning signal to avoid serious decisions.

## CONTRA-INDICATIONS TO DECISION-MAKING (DANGER TIME)

If you are suffering from any of the ailments or conditions described below, resist the urge to decide issues of importance regardless of external or internal pressures on you. Take refuge in deferral, procrastination, sloth or downright bloody-mindedness, and put off choosing until you feel, and preferably others confirm, that the phase, state or condition has passed.

1. **Post-traumatic stress states** – these follow accidents or profound shocks. They can be long-lasting, and sometimes recurrent. While they persist, rational choice-making is in jeopardy.

2. **Bereavement sequels** – these periods of mourning hold particular decision-making dangers. Temporary delusions about the deceased's wishes, or desires to recompense the dead, can destroy judgement, and are typical sequel-phenomena.

3. **For women, post and pre-menstrual cycle states**, especially if they have been associated with excitement or mood swings, are hazardous. Waiting a few days for such states to clear can be a valuable delay. There is also some decision-making risk in the early phase of menopause, particularly if mood changes are marked.

   **Pregnancy and post-pregnancy** are also times when women should be wary about deciding issues of significance. The reasons are plain. Many pregnancies are accompanied by untypical (but useful) feelings of euphoria which may not match reality. Some pregnancies are followed by unwelcome depressions, equally untypical.

4. **Post-operative periods** – the decisional risk here lies not so much in the physical shock of an operation but in the psychological consequences of anaesthetics. These can produce profound, but not always recognisable, personality changes that can take months to readjust or stabilise. Such periods are highly risky for personal decision-making.

5. **Post-influenza conditions** – influenza is especially crucial, but all sequel states to high fevers are potentially dangerous. Certain influenza virus strains can leave a sufferer with severe

depression or anxiety, or both. Consequent on the inertia the illness brings, **there may also be a paradoxical drive to action after the acute phase**. Couple these two factors, decision-wise, and all the ingredients of disaster are to hand.

6. **Seasonal affective disorder (SAD)** – sometimes termed 'hibernation sickness' from its apparent association with the sleep and activity diminishment of some mammals and reptiles, seasonal affective disorder is an important contra-indicator for decisions of any significance.

It typically begins in November, or early December, with drastic curtailment of daylight. At the beginning, the symptoms resemble influenza with aching joints followed by an intense, generalised feeling of irritability. The sufferer experiences sensations of cold; shivering bouts are common and depression grows. Weight-gain is a defining characteristic. It begins almost at once, as if to model the fat-accumulation common to many hibernating animals, and thus distinguishes SAD from depression, in which weight stays steady or is lost.

The majority of SAD sufferers, estimated at 2 to 3 per cent of the population, develop some insight into their condition. They realise that for at least three, and possibly four, winter months, their relationships with others are likely to be under tension, and their judgement across a range of situations will be significantly impaired. The task for this group, as for other categories of sufferers in this section, is to put off choices for the duration. For SAD prone, however, the no-choosing or deciding period is typically and crucially longer.

7. **Disorientation** (see especially Chapter 9, impulse decisions) – being securely orientated, i.e. feeling familiar, accepted and poised in a setting where a decision may have to be made, is an essential requirement for rational thinking and acting. A sense of strangeness, or alienation from self or surroundings or both, can create an irresistible urge to escape often translated into self-destructive, almost reflex actions.

Our case history in Chapter 9 focuses upon a disorientated student at university. It would be an error, however, to conclude that this factor relates exclusively to immature young persons at college. Any fresh setting imposes an element of disorientation: holidays, especially foreign ones, hospitalisation, etc., whether **benign** or **threatening**, **sought** or **imposed** by circumstances. If you find yourself in a situation of strangeness, beware of deciding anything of significance, until such time as your feeling of alienation has passed, or you return to familiar surroundings.

Obviously there are variations in the severity of all these states and conditions, and their personal impacts. But deferring a decision is usually not difficult, and if you are in any doubt about your circumstantial judgement it is far safer to put off making up your mind until you are really sure.

## Examples of ill-timed decisions

Tragically, people *do* decide important, even vital, issues in states where making choices is very ill-advised. Over the years your author has noted the following:

- A widow who was so impressed by her husband's death-bed preoccupation with a religious cult he had previously hardly noticed that, despite no mention or bequest in his will, she handed over the bulk of his estate to it, and reduced herself to penury for the rest of her life.

- A professional woman who suffered a botched operation for a riding accident which necessitated a five-hour anaesthetic. A month after surgery, she walked out on her husband of fifteen years, her children and her job, left the country and never came back.

- An apparently loving and caring professional couple with two children and an assured community status who were involved in a serious coach accident. Some months later they split up and then were divorced.

- A young mother on maternity leave but suffering from the 'baby-blues' who, hearing some work-gossip, (it was quite inaccurate), sent in her notice, and took two years to secure another job.

## Raising awareness – for self and others

How can we be sure of realising that we're not in the right state to make good decisions?

- Making a brief list of prompts (the contra-indications described above) and fixing this in strategic places (medicine cupboard, family diary, wardrobe door) is a very useful awareness-raising device, both for ourselves and others.

- Not being reticent about discussing our feelings in such states with others.

- Occasionally reviewing our memories of emotions experienced in such states.

- Keeping a watch on close others who may be at risk from contra-indications.

It is all too simple to overlook the decisional significance of any state we may be in; as if there were a cut-off mechanism at work, which by focusing attention on immediate circumstances (principally the tasks of stabilising ourselves or getting well) deprives us of the necessary warning insight.

### Ignoring the warning signs
I have a trivial but, at the same time, striking example of how effective such a 'cut-off mechanism' can be. Since the age of 15 I have been aware that the period before lunch is a critical, emotional, phase for me. I am very liable to lose my temper, become suddenly depressed, or attempt some task for which there is insufficient time. My mother's profound observation, 'a hungry man is an angry man', shared by my current womenfolk, has ensured that I am swiftly fed, whereupon I usually recover my emotional balance. Providentially, I do not recall making any decisions in this hungry/angry state (blood-sugar levels drop sharply before meals and the brain suffers). Intriguingly, however, I have *never yet* recognised its causal significance at the time, even though I must have experienced it on numerous occasions. Only afterwards do I realise that, once again, I have let my blood-sugar levels fall, and my temper take over.

### Understanding the effects of mental illness
The above is an example of a physiological condition. Paradoxically, however, serious psychological illness (anxiety, depression or compulsion states) can produce a phenomenon termed **neurotic indecision**. Here we see a situation somewhat different from deferred choice where the onus to decide is on the chooser. In effect we have choices which should be made being blocked by the emotional illness. The phenomenon is close but not equivalent to the **parity**

**problem** category (see pages 109 and 110). The sufferer is inhibited from deciding because of illness-reduced concentration and confused motivation, coupled with a tendency to exaggerate the consequences of decisional errors. Thus the sufferer is left in a precarious limbo, facing decisional demands which he/she cannot, for the duration of the illness, meet.

## EXERCISE 8.1

Refer to the list of contra-indications above, in particular nos. 1–6. Search your experience and identify a decision taken in a contra-indicated state which proved regrettable. It should be a significant decision, but need not necessarily have been *your* decision.

(a)  Describe the state.

(b)  Detail the circumstances of the decision.

(c)  Account, as far as possible, for the subject's failure to delay his/her decision.

(d)  Describe the outcome, and whether the adverse consequences were retrievable.

## UNDERSTANDING INSUFFICIENCY

We are now moving away from the 'shouldn't' to the 'couldn't' and 'wouldn't' conditions of decision-taking, where forms of calculation rule. They loom especially important in business settings, as the next case study confirms, but they feature also in personal lives, being much involved with intimate values and feelings. If they have a common sub-factor it is that, regardless of deliberate calculation, they all generate a measure of anxiety insofar as they all denote uncertainty.

### Case study: Marian worries about the risks of cancer

Marian was Product Research Director of one of the country's largest cosmetic firms, and in a quandary of considerable dimensions. In front or her was the laboratory report on the firm's new anti-wrinkle lotion, and it posed a dilemma only she could resolve. The lotion was certainly not toxic, in the sense of its causing dermatitis, but the risk of its being carcinogenic remained uncalculated, on account of the difficulty of running suitable animal skin trials.

Marian knew that none of the chemicals in the lotion had ever been incriminated as carcinogenic, either separately or in previous lotion formulae. But, and it was a but that grew bigger as one pondered on it, there was that short article in the *International Journal of Cosmetics Technology*, last month. It had come from a French laboratory, and pinpointed a very small risk of cancer in laboratory guinea pigs with one of the new continental formulations for a similar lotion, using well tried, 'safe' chemicals.

Marian decided not to decide. She scribbled a memo to Tom, the Product Director:

'Tom,' (it read) 'I know you're desperate to set up on AW 204 but we simply cannot move until the cancer trials are run. The court awards for company liability are too horrendous. I'll hurry them up, but I dare not force them to skimp. Can you give me six months, or will Concos pip us to the launch?'

### Analysing the case study

How should we analyse Marian? One useful method, yielding qualitative and quantitative insights as necessary, is to produce the categories or **ownership** and **implications**.

- By **ownership** we mean the degree to which the decision-maker possesses his/her decision, and further commands it. Status, personal initiative and style are but three of the factors in ownership, which is a complex entity.

- **Implications** are to a limited degree subordinate to ownership, but also have interpretational values that stretch much further. Implications wrap together time-schemes, risk possibilities, uncertainties, unpredictable behaviour of others, demands on the skills of the decision-maker, etc., in a bundle that differs in composition from one deferred decision to the next.

How then does Marian's deferred decision stand in terms of ownership and implications?

### Analysing ownership

There is no doubt that Marian owns this decision, and does so by virtue of her company status and responsibilities. Nobody else comes close to her in terms of possession. She identified the problem and has shaped it to suit her own constructs. She will decide the factors to unlock the decision to defer.

## Analysing the implications

We perceive a clutch of implications, some of which may test Marian's judgement and professionalism to the utmost degree. **Time** is of the first essence. Can adequate, and the emphasis is on adequate, **data** be gathered up in time to meet the production schedule? Can more be discovered of the credibility of that French research? How fast and far can the in-house research be pushed before it ceases to be reliable? What if this in-house work still returns uncertain data? To what degree could such work, if honestly conducted, be considered to relieve her firm of **liability**, and how might it be presented to any court of law? Although there seems a solid ownership, could it crumble if Tom, himself pressurised, **leans** on her, or has others do the leaning, and she is forced against her better judgement to allow the lotion into production?

**External factors** could, of course, intervene in unforeseen or half-foreseen ways. Changes in product safety legislation could alter the risk criteria surrounding all cosmetics testing, making standards tighter and penalties more severe.

We could continue with this list and, if space allowed, set it out in order of likelihood and significance. But even at this length it is clear that serious decisions, deferred on grounds of unsufficiency, with considerable ownership for their makers, can be very stress-provoking, and can test nerve and judgement to the utmost.

## HANDLING THE PARITY PROBLEM

On first study, a deferral because one cannot evaluate and choose between different options might seem to be another form of insufficiency. It would be an error to conclude this – the roots of a parity problem do not usually lie in a lack of information, but in a **failure of processing**. Such failures can be traced to various causes, but **confused values** or **distorted attitudes** are frequently involved, as in the following case study.

### Case study: Melissa juggles with Paul and Geoff

Melissa's parity problem focused deliciously on two men, and her inability to decide which of them to live with, if either. There was Paul, thirtyish, trim, with his kit off, even trimmer, successful travel agent, owner of a second-hand Porsche with a terrifying roll-cage, possessor of a pine double-bed, oversize to sixty-five inches, amusing, very, very exciting, but a man you had to watch.

And then there was Geoff, thirtyish also, who could have been trim had he taken himself in hand, supervisor at a local drop-in centre, owner of a second-hand Raleigh bicycle, short of lights, possessor of a put-u-up settee, made circa 1959, attentive, sympathetic, but attractively in need of mothering.

Keeping two men in the air was a juggling act that needed all Melissa's skills. But sorting out her feelings was quite beyond her. Sex with Paul was a thrilling battle in which you grabbed every bit of buzz that came your way. With Geoff, love-making was more akin to nursing. He needed to prove himself every time; you had to top up his confidence.

Paul said that she reminded her of Liz Hurley. Geoff found her as soothing as the honey, he claimed, she was named for. Melissa soon stopped telling them about each other. Frowns and silences always followed. A woman had to think about the future. How long would someone as moneyed and attractive as Paul want her? Would he ever come to need her? And could she hope to get a hold over him?

Getting a hold over Geoff would be no problem. But whether it would be a satisfying grip in the long run was more uncertain. Would she be dragged into a dependency relationship? Did one grow into a dominating role?

Melissa's grandmother, aged 87, was not overhelpful. 'What you need is a good hiding,' she said, lovingly.

**Analysing ownership**

However she may judge her circumstances, objectively Melissa's ownership of this decision is very questionable, and could be contested at any time. She has no status, beyond that of an attractive, nubile woman, and only limited leverage, and the very real problem of the caprice of two men, to tackle and resolve. There is much that is open-ended and untidy about the whole situation; perhaps it is the very uncertainty of the affairs that is holding this framework of tenuous relationships together. At the moment when certainty touches any of the protagonists, the structure may well collapse.

**Analysing the implications**

Melissa is not clear on what she wants or needs and the options she perceives do not help to crystallise her objectives. The two men are polarised as personality types. Even on the relative common ground of sexual pleasures, they deliver and she enjoys significantly different thrills. Once away from bed, and she is stretched precariously to accommodate herself to their diverse values and lifestyles. If they reflect the two sides of her nature, and this may not be its totality, unless one or other broadens his attitude so that he can satisfy her across the full range of her needs, the impasse will continue.

But common sense tells us that it will not continue indefinitely. In fact, the timescale for her deferred decision is much narrower and more complex than either Melissa or her lovers could imagine. She may be deluding herself if she thinks that she has all the time in the world to make up her mind. Sex has its own rhythms and seasons. Suppose jealousy invades the situation? Consider the possibilities that Melissa may quarrel seriously with one, and then find herself unacceptable to the other. Threesomes have peculiar and unstable dynamics; sometimes they may be invaded and consequently destabilised by fourth parties.

This gives some possible pointers as to how Melissa's decisional dilemma may be resolved. If she retains ownership the solution may lie in emotional quadratic equations – the entry of another man who straddles her needs, obscure to her as they may continue to be. But her lovers may also solve their own quadratic equations by choosing for permanent partners young women who can make up their minds.

## KEEPING THE OPTIONS OPEN

On first analysis, deferring our decision in order to keep our options open seems to rest on a set of confident certainties. We have appraised the situation with its offers and prospects: we are sure of our own abilities; all the inherent risks of deferral have been assessed; the entire context is known and owned. But, just as we are excluding insufficiency of information as a possible factor in 'options open', it enters via the back door. **For we may well be deciding to keep our options open out of ignorance of where our best interests lie!**

### Case study: Kevin receives an interesting offer

When the Managing Director offered him the leadership of the Dispatch Department, Kevin said nothing and just looked pleased. 'I expect you'd like a bit of time to consider,' the Managing Director said. 'How long is it open?' Kevin enquired. 'Well,' said the Managing Director, 'I don't want to run right up to Philip's retirement. We've got to give ourselves a bit to time for an easy take-over.' 'Can you keep it open for two months?' Kevin asked. 'Two months, but not a day more,' the Managing Director said, not too warmly. Two months, Kevin thought, two months. In two months we will know if Ellis is coming back. Radiotherapy is always a hit-

and-miss business, but two months should sort it out somehow. And if he doesn't come back, I'm sitting pretty in the Section, having been carrying the load for a year. Far better to step into Ellis's shoes than blunder into the shambles that Philip's made of Dispatch.

### Analysing ownership

A confident operator, this Kevin, but is he over-confident in his ownership of this decision? In status terms such ownership must be questionable. He does not possess the Managing Director's clout, nor does he have any control over whether Ellis, his present superior, will have the chance to return to work. His leverage depends on assumptions, and his decision when he makes it will succeed or fail as much on account of what he is assuming, or risking, as what he believes he knows.

### Analysing the implications

Time-schemes may be crucial in this deferral, so we should consider them carefully. If Ellis does not come back to work within the MD's offer period, and more important, is reliably reported to be still ailing, Kevin will pass up the chance of heading-up Dispatch. He will then confidently expect to succeed Ellis. But his confidence could be misplaced. The MD might well appoint over his head, perhaps out of pique at being thwarted on the Philip move, or possibly because he wishes to keep Kevin for another trouble-shooting role elsewhere. Then there is the possible knock-on effect of Kevin's deferral on Ellis. Learning that Kevin is playing artful games may conceivably motivate Ellis towards a genuine health improvement, or at least a mischievous string of statements that he hopes soon to be back at work. By this means he may rid himself of a troublesome assertive deputy who will be compelled to accept the MD's offer. Again, the effect of deferral on others cannot be underestimated. The MD's pique at being refused an immediate decision might extend to setting-up open interviews for Philip's post. Kevin would, of course, be the preferred candidate. But we've probably all heard of similar open-and-shut selections where matters have gone very awry for seeming favourite sons or daughters and, where to their rage and chagrin, they have been passed over for outsiders.

Does Kevin have a fall-back position for his deferred decision? Could he be said to have planned any contingent strategy to limit the damage should his scheme run into difficulty? It would seem that he could in certain circumstances be awkwardly placed, particularly if Ellis comes back, for a limited period, and Kevin is locked into Philip's Dispatch role, and unable to transfer back when Ellis finally goes. He may then belatedly discover that deputising for Ellis in a relatively soft section is no training for the large demands that straightening out the Philip muddle will make.

## EXAMINING DEFECTIVE STYLE

Kevin's story serves to show that of the three deferral modes, insufficiency, parity problem and options open, the third is much the riskiest.

- There is an all-or-nothing quality to **insufficiency**; either we get what we need, or we do not move.

- With **parity problem**, the prospect of intervening circumstances, of some shift in emphasis or value on the part of the decision-maker or another, offers a good prospect of the deadlock being broken.

- But **options open** frequently and riskily involves the deferrer in tight time-schemes, questionable assumptions of the motives of others and, perhaps most crucially, the chance that the very act of keeping an option open will be misinterpreted negatively, or generate self-assertive and, therefore, obstructive acts by those the deferrer most needs to remain passive, pliant or predictable.

## EXERCISE 8.2

Refer to the three categories of deferred decision: insufficiency, parity problem and options open. Search your experience and identify a deferred decision of yours in any one of those categories.

(a) Describe the decisional situation.

(b) Analyse it, using the ownership and implications categories.

(c) Indicate the outcome and the success or otherwise of the deferral process.

# 9
# Avoiding Impulse Decision-Making

An **impulse decision** is a choice based predominantly on emotions, where facts and consequences play little or no part. Such actions, driven by **feelings**, whether isolated, occasional or part of a lifestyle pattern controlled by irresistible urges, must *all* be seen as potentially hazardous for the impulse decision-maker.

## FACING DECISION-MAKING CHALLENGES

There are three broad **categories** of challenge in impulse decision, and they form the structure of this chapter.

- The first comprises the **vulnerable**, defined as those who are placed in disorientating and/or threatening circumstances in which inexperience and unsupported emotional needs make impulses irresistible in terms of their self-control.

- The second is a more general category of those who **fail to understand their own motivations or refine their aims**, and consequently are unable to make rational decisions based on facts. Deprived of processing skills, they fall victim to whim and fantasy.

- The third, and most tragic category, exclusively comprises the **chronic impulse-prone**. These are those who have never developed mature control of instinctual response and are thus at the mercy of any event which triggers aggressive, acquisitive, evasive, appetitive or habit-formed behaviour.

## CATEGORY 1: ISOLATED BUT CRUCIAL IMPULSE DECISIONS

Not every decision taken on impulse can be seen as part of a familiar pattern of behaviour. Sometimes they occur as isolated, once-and-for-all acts, never or seldom repeated in a lifetime. Sadly, however, their singularity may bear no relation to their significance. They may occur once, but once too often. This is particularly the case with the isolated impulse decision, often taken by a young person, which can have life-long consequences.

## Case study: Jack drops out

Jack was stunned when the Cambridge college offered him a place to read philosophy and art history. Nobody in his family had ever been to university before. Cambridge was 200 miles distant and apart from a trip to Florida with his aunt and uncle when he was fifteen, he had never been away from home. But he was more than stunned when he went up; he was terrified. Everyone he met was appallingly smart, clever and well-connected. A young woman undergraduate on the next staircase was a niece of the Prime Minister. The man sharing his room had a clarinet, and practised modern pieces of awesome complexity. And Jack was homesick; more achingly and confusingly homesick than he could have believed. He listened at night to the trains roaring north, and wished he was on one, homeward bound.

On his third evening, Jack went along to the Aesthetics Society. The talk, given by an Oxford academic of international repute, was on the narrative contributions of Derrida. The content was double Dutch or, more properly, French to Jack and most of the audience, but not to one elegant and intense young man who rose at question time and tore the lecturer's thesis to pieces. He even locked into a textual tangle with the lecturer and floored him with an exquisitely delivered quotation from Derrida himself. Nobody told Jack that Cambridge is a poseur's paradise, but in the end even the most inflated reputations are cut down to size.

Next morning Jack rose, had breakfast in hall, packed his suitcases, ordered a taxi to the station, and never went back.

Of course, we do not know what happened to Jack subsequently. Perhaps he decided against higher education and sought a job. It's a mystery. But we can be sure of one outcome: that decision, taken on impulse, must have altered his life significantly, and perhaps reduced his chances. Yet there was nothing inevitable about his dropping out. Forethought on his, his parents', the college authorities' and the university's part could have prevented this personal crisis.

Suppose we reduce his problems to the following set of categories:

- **disorientation** – feeling of strangeness, isolation

- **homesickness** – irresistible longing for familiar surroundings
- **sense of inferiority** – shock of comparing himself with others.

There are ways of tackling all these stress factors. Some require forethought, others can be addressed as they appear.

### Tackling disorientation
The army has a maxim, true for all human predicaments: **time spent on reconnoitring is never wasted**. Jack should have been up visiting the college several times before the start of term, getting the feel, poking his nose into its odd corners, reading the old JCR notices, exploring the University as a whole, discovering its facilities and opportunities. Any chance encounter should have been used ruthlessly. (I found out more about the college I – unsuccessfully! – targeted there during a ten-minute walk from the station with an older student, than from any amount of information sent to me.)

Jack should have tried to spend a night at the college or, failing that, the YMCA. He should have sought to pin his prospective tutor down (ever elusive people) and/or secured a reading list. And, if possible, he should have come up the day before the official start of term. Even if you are fresh, it's just as well to be in position, before everybody appears. If there had been any current or past Cambridge students in his home town, Jack should have been badgering them for information, gossip or views. All this effort would not have been in vain, if it meant that he arrived with a feeling, however slight, of familiarity.

### Preventing homesickness
Jack's parents were responsible for this factor. They should have arranged and insisted that he spend at least a month free of family away from home. This experience, ideally at age 16 or 17, will usually be sufficient to desensitize the average adolescent against separation anxiety.

### Overcoming a sense of inferiority
This is a near universal potential stress factor in students. A precocious display of competence in French philosophy is not essential for its emergence – almost any perceived or imagined deficiency will do. Young people who have not been challenged by local competition may possess a certain confidence, but its falsity may be revealed when up against displays of exceptional ability. They may be plunged into despondency, and if such descents

happen at crucial times, tempted to act impulsively, irrationally and irretrievably. It is at these critical moments that they require skilled help, the kind of counselling support that all university counselling services are on hand to supply. Tragically, it is sometimes not just a question of dropping-out, serious though that decision may be. A trapped student, squeezed between needs and demands, may decide to end it all by suicide.

The question arises, however, as to who takes the initiative in seeking out counselling. Does Jack search it out for himself? If he does, how does he decide that he needs help? This raises an immensely important decisional issue, dealt with to some degree in another section of this book. Perhaps Jack is advised by the college to go to the Counselling Service. But this implies that it has put in place a system of immediate, personal tutoring.

On my third day at Oxford, I was asked by my moral tutor (the most celebrated philosopher of our age) whether I was frustrated. 'Of course,' I replied, playing it clever. In fact, I was in a state of excited terror caused by my perception that my fellow students universally outshone me in terms of height, looks, health, wealth, talent, charm and experience.

## EXERCISE 9.1

Refer to page 114 (isolated but crucial impulse decisions). Review your personal history. Write a confidential anecdote describing any circumstances in which *you* have come close to an impulse decision which might have had critical consequences. Give details of the setting, the pressures on you, the help you had to withstand them or otherwise, and the urges you eventually overcame. Also outline the possible outcomes had you yielded to an impulse at that time.

## CATEGORY 2: FAILURE TO CLARIFY GOALS OR UNDER-STAND MOTIVATIONS

The people who fall into this category are not necessarily immature, unsupported or unprepared. They are defined, however, by two characteristics: their failure to clarify personal goals, and typically also to understand their deeper motivations.

People in this category come to grief in a range of different activities. We can observe their disasters in social, personal, occupational and physical contexts. But business is where their failure seems most obvious.

## Impulse decisions in business settings

The burdensome paraphernalia of finance-raising, market-research-ing, planning and projecting might seem to exclude the possibility that impulse could play a dominant part in business decision-making. But this would be an illusion. 'Leaping before looking' or, more realistically, 'leaping after a frustrating bout of looking has made *not* leaping somehow unbearable' is a familiar introduction to business grief, and could be traced as a significant cause of failure in a variety of enterprises. Take the case of Emma.

## Case study: Emma fails the hygiene inspection

Thinking about it afterwards, Emma concluded that her biggest mistake had been to want to run her own business without a clear idea of what that business might be. She was thirty, single, still living at home with her parents, and possessed of an irresistible urge to manage her own shop or café. But what and where, to say nothing of how, were still deliciously mysterious in her mind. Clearly, it had to be a small venture; her resources, to say nothing of her skills, would not stretch to anything elaborate, but whether it should be a fancy boutique, gift shop, little hardware store or a café where burgers were flipped, or whatever, was unclear and unexplored.

One afternoon she was strolling down Albion Street, an alley close to the station, when she saw a shop to let, and 'lease for sale' sign above a small café. It was a grotty hash-house in a none-too-prosperous location, but there were customers within, and possibles passing, so almost on impulse she went in. The proprietor (he seemed to be single-handed) was stacking plates, toasting sandwiches and taking money simultaneously. He handed Emma a leaflet in response to her enquiry which read:

> **HELLO BUYER**, your opportunity! I want to dispose of the lease on The Hot Spot which, as you can see, is very much a going concern. As of this month all I ask is £4,500 for the remainder of the eight-month period, and £500 for the goodwill and fittings. If you are looking for a bargain, and are not afraid of hard work, please bother the chef at the servery.

Emma gazed about her. Two more customers had just come in, and were at the servery bar. A thrilling sensation of possessing, managing, of being independent, and on her own, started to fill her. It was almost a sexual buzz; she felt suddenly warmer, and at least 50 per cent more alive. Holding the leaflet she went up to the servery bar.

The chef, owner, bottle-washer and sandwich toaster looked both harassed and uneasy. 'I'll give you a look round,' he offered, 'But there's not much more to see.'

That was an understatement. Apart from a damp storeroom with a freezer and a rusty gas cooker and an even damper toilet with a chain flush, there was little else. 'What's the reason to sell?' Emma asked. The owner looked even more uneasy. 'I've had an offer,' he said. 'Chef-courier on the biggest holiday cruiser in the Aegean. Linking the cuisine afloat with island restaurants. It's the chance of a lifetime.'

Emma was most impressed. The café seemed to suddenly take on an exotic atmosphere. She could almost hear Greek music. 'One thing,' she asked, 'Will I get the lease renewed?' 'Renewed?' the owner almost hooted. 'I'll say he'll renew it, probably halve it, he's that desperate. And you should clear enough in eight months to take care of any new lease.'

A health and safety worry prompted Emma. The storeroom and toilet were clearly outside regulations. 'What's the estimate to refurbish this to hygiene standards?' she asked. The proprietor looked more and more uneasy. 'About two grand,' he said, adding, 'but don't fret, my brother-in-law's on the Health Committee. The word in Public Health according to him is, keep your heads down. Nobody's ever come round.' '*I'll* be lucky,' Emma thought to herself. 'I'm due for some luck; I will be able to put enough aside to cover the fresh lease, and possibly a bit more, in case they check up next year.'

'I need five thousand pounds,' Emma told the bank manager, hoping that so small a loan would prompt him to offer her more. But bank managers are alert to such ploys; they have one thing only on their minds, security, and this Emma could scarcely offer at all. The manager asked her what her start-up expenditure was, and on learning that the lease to expiry was almost the sum requested, grew warier than ever.

'Five thousand will be the limit,' he said, 'and that's against my better judgement, because you're not allowing anything for contingencies.' Three days into the venture with business promising rather than surging, a pleasant-looking man came up to the counter and showed Emma an identity card from the Public Health Department. 'I though you wouldn't be bothering us,' Emma said, lamely. 'Sorry, but we're having a bit of a blitz,' the pleasant-looking man said. 'There's been a red-hot circular from the Department of Health.'

When he left after half-an-hour, he gave Emma a notice. It allowed her fourteen days to begin refurbishing the storeroom and toilet; failing compliance, the café would close.

## Analysing Emma's mistakes

Emma's fundamental error was a failure to define her **goals** to herself, or to seek the kind of expert help which might have clarified them. Shaping goals, particularly on your own, is not easy. There are, however, some useful characterising features to be borne in mind:

1.  Goals should relate to results and products rather than the actions or plans that generate them.

2.  Goals should not be vague.

3.  Goals should create substantial challenges.

4.  Goals should be realistically achievable.

5.  There should be sufficient time for goals to be attained.

6.  Goals should match the values of the goal-setter.

Let's use these criteria to examine how Emma measured up, giving her a score out of 10 in each case.

1.  She was clearly much more interested in activities than products. Self-display, independence and prestige all took precedence over customer satisfaction or even profit. There was no clear linkage in her mind between achievement and methods. **3/10**

2.  Emma's goals were vague to the point of non-existence. She could not frame or shape them, either to herself or others. This left her at the mercy of any plausible-seeming offer or passing whim. **3/10**

3.  The vague and diffuse goals that Emma had were not capable of creating a realistic challenge that she could respond to with tough-minded planning, analysis and judgement. **2/10**

4. Even in terms of her vague goals Emma did not make realistic plans. She took serious, whim-driven risks on the flimsiest of assurances, and against her deeper judgement. **4/10**

5. Emma does not appear to have set herself any time limits at all. This is a very serious, self-imposed, handicap liable to result in being overwhelmed by a 'spasm to choose' without being able to block it temporarily with a timetable objection. **2/10**

6. We do not know much about Emma's values, but we sense some mismatch between the two systems. Values run very close to needs, and if they are not in close alignment, the 'spasm to choose' may be impossible to control. **3/10**

## Looking at things differently

How might a clear framework of **goals** and **aims** have helped Emma avoid being overwhelmed by an impulse to be in business at any cost? Let's suppose that she had:

• set herself long rather than short-term objectives

• carefully analysed at least one alternative business possibility, even fast-food

• realised that the reluctance of the bank manager to advance her a sizeable loan was based on business judgement not personal prejudice.

• had developed some insight into the degree to which she was in a state of decisional instability.

## Getting some business counselling

If anybody was/is in need of business counselling it is/was Emma. All aspects of her complex but essentially solvable problem demand skilled attention. She requires a thorough-going, problem-solving approach, directive rather than reflective, focused rather than holistic. She should receive:

• help with **self-discovery**, of motivations, interests, aptitudes and available or trainable skills

• guidance on the assessment and gathering-up of **resources**

• help with the methodology of **prospect analysis**, market research, and business planning

- **support** in the crucial initial stages of her venture.

She needs many sessions with such a business counsellor, and much opportunity for meditation, discussion with others, legwork, fieldwork and homework. Let us hope that before she ventures again, she seeks it out.

### EXERCISE 9.2

Try to put yourself in the position of a business counsellor tackling Emma's venture problem.

(a) Develop a scheme to sort out her short- and long-term objectives.
(b) Devise a method for comparing and analysing two alternative business possibilities.

You may find Chapter 6 of use in this exercise.

### CATEGORY 3: THE CHRONIC IMPULSE-PRONE

This is the most demanding of our management challenges, in terms of both size and potential for growth. As I have been writing this book, I have been reading of a new impulse phenomenon, the **consumerist**, who cannot control expenditure, and is driven into debt and despair by an insatiable desire to buy and buy. In our image-ridden and statement-making society, this problem can be expected to grow.

#### Losing the freedom to choose

In some sense the impulse consumer, and similarly every other sufferer whose judgement is overwhelmed by uncontrollable drives or desires, has lost the freedom to choose. In its place a mechanical apparatus has been substituted, keeping them in an automatic, robotic servitude. Theirs is joint slavery: to the **cue**, happening, stimulus or event that triggers the impulse mechanism, and also to the **emotional surge** that powers it.

This cue-to-impulse mechanism is a complicated system. A helpful analogy is a bird snatching a fish from water. In this model the bird is the occasional, precisely provoking stimulus, the fish an impulse or decisive feeling rising to the surface of consciousness. Unless the bird is well positioned and its prey near the surface, a satisfying meal is unlikely to be the product of this encounter. Similarly, in the reality of the sufferer's life, there may be many occasions when either:

- the appropriate releasing circumstances are present, but the impulse to be released is weak, *or*

- the feelings are strong, but no releasing factors present themselves.

Like life itself, and the fishing experience of birds, the whole process is a hit-and-miss affair. But the important lesson this analogy teaches is that of the interlocking nature of occasional circumstances. Impulse-prone personalities are in the grip of psychological interlock. Their lives are decisional disasters waiting to happen, whenever mood and cue match fatally together.

### Understanding the psychological factors

If impulsive decisions (choices made on whim, options closed for irrational reasons) lead to personal disasters and distorted lives, why do prone personalities continue with such self-destructive behaviour?

Several complex psychological reasons have been advanced to answer this obvious but none-the-less pointed question. Most persuasive is the undoubted fact that many decisions taken on impulse are very **pleasurable** at the time of taking, and remain so in retrospect even though their consequences may have been painful. Many such decisions ride upon the strongest possible flood of **instinctual emotion**, a guarantee of good feeling. For the impulse-prone personality especially, another mechanism comes into play when the pleasure is subsequently punished by consequences. Having one's **pleasure punished** is a secondary 'pleasure' for sufferers such as these, but an important reinforcing one.

Another more general reinforcement may occur when, as very **occasionally** happens, the impulse decision is **justified by results**. All humankind (and the animal kingdom too) is reinforced behaviourally by intermittent success. This is an essential survival mechanism; without it life would not be motivated to try, try and try again.

And then from a wider survival standpoint we should briefly consider why, if impulsive behaviour is so self-defeating, it has not been eliminated by the inexorable processes of evolution. To understand why, we must see at least some impulsive behaviour as possessing **survival value**, as balancing an evolutionary tendency to *overcivilise* humankind. Genetically we may need the input that impulsive choices bring – the thoughtless unions, the disruptive acts – because only they can painfully provide the variety our human race needs to survive the challenges of the world.

## Understanding the effects

The predicament of the **impulse-prone personality** (IPP) is serious. IPP behaviour is not a once-and-for-all yielding to impulse, or an occasional isolated lapse, it is a repetitive lifestyle of responding to instinctual challenges with a variety of unacceptable, self-defeating acts. IPP typically leads to **isolation**, **restraint by others** and, variously, **degradation** because social norms and legal codes are continuously being flouted and broken. **Personal relationships** are inevitably damaged; parents, siblings, children, spouses and colleagues find IPP behaviour intolerable, and shun the sufferer. IPP behaviour is also often complicated by **compulsion** – typically the sufferer is also habit-prone. Pilfering or addictions to drink or drugs compensate for the pain and guilt which result from the impulsive decisions made.

## A psychological framework

IPP psychology is not simple, but the theoretical framework appears to indicate that:

1. The sufferer has little insight, and does not recognise the shape of situations which in the past have triggered impulsive decisions.

2. The sufferer has been deprived of early training in self-control.

3. The sufferer does not grasp that a repertoire of responses (including no response at all) is available to every decisional event.

4. The sufferer does not comprehend that human beings are capable of deliberation, i.e. that there is a gap between stimulus-to-action and action itself, which judgement fills in balanced personalities.

5. Yielding to an impulse is a pleasurable act, which, occasionally repeated, creates a reinforcing effect on its own terms. Impulse decisions which are, even more rarely, successful in their outcomes are also a reinforcement.

6. Sufferers need, but seldom secure, skilled psychotherapeutic help. Reflective counselling is of little value. By contrast, cognitive-behavioural techniques, which sensitize them to recognise the semi-automatic process at work in themselves, offer the best prospect.

## Getting help

There is a range of approaches, but common features are as follows:

• Ensuring that the sufferer gains some **insight** into his or her condition. This can be done by means of autobiographical exercises: the sufferer is encouraged to write or record a detailed account of his or her personal history with particular reference to those emotional states and surrounding circumstances which provoked past impulsive acts. The purpose of such exercises is, of course, to build up the sufferer's powers of identification so that he or she can recognise the cues for impulsive acts before the cues take over the action. Day-by-day diaries may also be kept to obtain a more detailed account of the cycles of feelings in the sufferer's everyday life.

• When sufficient enabling insight is gained, therapy then moves on to providing the sufferer with a **response kit**, i.e a carefully prearranged and rehearsed set of problem-solving techniques designed to create considered or deferred decisions in circumstances which hitherto produced only impulsive actions.

## Practising the techniques

Acting instinctively can be deeply ingrained so counter-instinctual behaviour has to be taught and practised until it is virtually automatic. This is as much cognitive as emotive learning and, in terms of the former, several ingenious techniques have been pressed into service by therapists. **Chess playing**, for example, is a very useful forethought exercise. If a sufferer can think four or five moves ahead, it is possible that the variations implied can generalise to real-life situations where others may react to the sufferer's decisions. An even more important benefit could derive from the mere delay in response caused by the necessity to think the moves through. The simple but vital act of not responding immediately can allow the sufferer time to think, and in the interval more sophisticated and useful strategies can take hold.

## Rational-emotive approach

The approach of the rational-emotive psychologist to IPP is particularly relevant. This theory is based on the belief that:

• impulse response to events can be determined by semi-automatic thoughts, feelings and actions, based in part on

- false, self-defeating philosophies learned in early development, which can only be controlled by

- relearning the correct response and thereby modifying the feelings.

## Using coverants

A typical rational-emotive technique to gain control over impulsive urges and irrational feelings is the method of coverants. A coverant is a well-directed warning to the self of the dangers of yielding to a specific impulse. The warning takes the shape of a short statement, simple in content, focused in meaning.

For example: 'If you quit this job, you may never work again' is a strong **negative coverant**, directed at those who, for whatever insufficient reason, leave their employment. It is negative in that it emphasises the possible personal disaster that the impulse decision may provoke.

To be effective, however, coverants must also be **positive**. For example 'Stick with this job, and you will soon be out of debt' promises rather than threatens. It is the essential reverse coupled in sequence, one negative, the other positive.

## Blocking, and making space

Coverant control is a **blocking** technique. It is applied at the instant the sufferer feels the urge to impulsive action, immediately following the recognised stimulus or cue that summons up the feeling.

Coverant control is more than mere blocking, however. It aims for an **enlargement of decisional space and time**, that crucial interval between the realisation of an impending threatening impulse to irrational action and the action itself.

It is a crucial interval and coverants (they have to be introduced in multiple pairs, at least three to a set) are only one of a number of tactics designed to capitalise upon the precise point where trained willpower can have conclusive results. Coverants find a special role in **contracting systems** (described below). There are also simpler, less focused, activities not necessarily involving sub-vocal speaking, which can perform a more general blocking role. Examples are:

- **Counting mentally to a given number**, and then repeating. This can and should be varied considerably. Counting backwards from 50, counting backwards by odd numbers, or reciting sub-vocally the alphabet in reverse, are all useful variations.

- **Concentrating upon other cues**. This entails focusing upon a bodily process like breathing, measuring each breath; or generating a small regular movement with the foot, or fingers in pocket on which a continuous observation can be made.

- **The pain cue**. This is a deliberately induced discomfort (nail into palm, foot strained into tension, etc.) which pulls concentration away from immediate conflict considerations to the margin of events.

### Contracting systems

These are programmes of prearranged promises to the sufferer-self or to helpers/therapists, whereby the impulse-prone personality (IPP) is tied to a range of impulse-thwarting tactics, all designed to give him/her time for realistic thinking before reckless action. Contracts can be scheduled on a short- or long-term basis – weekly, monthly, yearly – and have penalty/reward features built into them. In the field of impulse decision-making management, the most informative examples of contracting systems lie in the habit domain, where the impulse is typically a frequent one, triggered by external and internal cues, and centred on addiction, alcoholism or gambling. In the very comprehensive contractual programme set out below, the focus is alcoholism, and the *impulse* is the devastating urge to drink.

### CONTRACT SCHEDULE

### Substitutes, Contracts, Distractions, Coverants, Activities and Interests Schedule to be completed weekly

　　　　　　　　　　　　End of week date.....................
1.  **Substitutes** (my substitutes this week) total.....................

2.  **Contracts**. I contracted £..... (state sum) for...................
    and won/lost (delete)

3.  **Distractions and stimuli**. I note the following alterations in stimuli for non-drinking...........................................

4.  **Coverants** I performed my coverant ....................... times
    　　　　　　 I missed my coverant ........................... times

5.  **Activities and interests** I maintained the following routine without a break ....................................................

Let us run through the strategies recommended.

## 1. Substitutes

What is a substitute? In part, heavy drinking is probably a substitutional activity. In the place of love, success, self-worth, the heavy drinker takes an excess of drink. So this section of the programme attempts to *substitute for the substitute*, i.e. that part of overdrinking that is related to the compulsive intake of fluids and solids, rather than the part that dulls the feelings of non-worth, etc. We recommend a range of liquid and solid substitutes to provide for this supping, chewing, swallowing, nibbling need. Soft drinks, chewing gum, mints, sweet and similar are comparatively harmless oral substitutes.

## 2. Contracts

Contracts and contracting is the method by which the alcoholic seeks to reduce his/her intake of alcohol, by a predetermined amount, and if successful, retrieves money placed in the trust of a friend. If, on the other hand, there is failure to meet targets, then the money is forfeit, with all the various aversive/inconvenient consequences that follow from the loss.

## 3. Distractions and stimuli

These are key aspects of the programme. An alcohol addict must reclaim and insulate himself/herself from the various stimuli that previously drew or cued drinking, and establish life in an environment where non-alcoholic stimuli predominate. It is particularly useful to know about different stimuli for drinking. We have noted some of them in the list below, together with the ways in which the alcoholic is conditioned so that a stimulus to drinking is followed by a drink. Such stimuli can be external or internal; for example, tension, anxiety or boredom (internal) or an offer of a drink or a business lunch (external) build a chain of circumstances which are likely to end in a drinking bout.

*Stimuli list*
1. I will not become involved in 'treating', knowing that this practice will increase my drinking.

2. I will acquaint myself with 'happy hour' times, in local public houses and hotels, so that I am not invited to patronise them during such times when drink is cheap.

3. I will 'taper' my relationships with drinking companions, so that I meet them out of drinking settings, and if they refuse to be thus 'tapered' I will drop them, and attempt to substitute other friends for them.

4. I will immediately switch off TV programmes in which drunkenness is 'laughed off' or minimised.

5. I will constantly challenge the profit-inspired doctrine that condones drinking and condemns drug-taking.

6. I will particularly sensitise myself to that point in the drinking process at which I lose control, and go on drinking.

7. I will not watch ITV (because drink-inducing advertisements are inevitable).

8. I will avoid the route/walk/part of the station, etc. which involves the hoarding where drink is brilliantly advertised.

9. I will *not* stray into the part of the supermarket/shop where drink is easy to buy, and if the arrangements are unavoidable, I will never patronise the shop again.

10. I will programme my day so that opportunities which may be filled in by drinking are avoided.

11. I will limit the contacts which I make during the day so that drinking proposals are neutralised.

12. I will programme my day so that I am *never* left alone with nothing to do but drink.

## Coverants

Coverant control of alcoholism is a method of self-instruction which involves the repetition of warning statements to the self or alternatively the deliberate, mental rehearsal of disagreeable fantasies. It follows a systematic method. The first stage for the self-manger is to keep a **record of drinking**, and impulses to drink, in a note book. This record must be maintained in the way set out in Figure 10. There should be sufficient number and spaces to show a full day's drinking urges, and actual drinks.

## Using statements

The next part of the sub-programme is the establishment of a **routine** whereby the drinker uses the urge to drink as a stimulus for coverant control of the drinking impulse. Put simply, on the

| **Drinking Schedule**<br>To be completed daily<br>Liquor only, not substitutes | |
| --- | --- |
| Date | |
| Amount drunk<br>Morning | |
| Amount drunk<br>Afternoon and<br>Evening | |
| Urges to drink<br>No. | |
| Intensity of urges<br>on scale least<br>to most 1–5 | |

Fig. 10. Drinking schedule.

realisation of an urge to drink, of whatever intensity, the drinker repeats sub-vocally an anti-drinking idea or **statement**, and immediately follows it with a pro-non-drinking statement.

The anti-drinking statement will relate to the dangers or social and personal disadvantages of drinking and the pro-non-drinking statement, the positive advantages of stopping drinking. Following the presentation of the second, pro-non-drinking statement, the self-manager **rewards** the coverant pair with the self-promise of a pleasurable event, other than a drink.

This coverant routine must become **automatic**, with the would-be non-drinker experiencing an impulse to drink, following that impulse immediately with an anti-drinking statement, dwelling on the anti-drinking statements, then turning instantly to the pro-non-drinking statement or idea, and finally moving on to the self-reward.

### Content of statements
The actual **content** of coverant statements has to be determined

precisely. The following are specimens of anti-drinking thoughts as self-statements:

- 'You will lose your job through drinking.'
- 'You will lose your driving licence through drinking.'

A large kit of comparable and possibly more individually appropriate statements should be developed on these models.

The following could be pro-non-drinking thoughts:

- 'You will be able to make love to your wife more effectively, if you stop drinking.'
- 'You will be able to play games more enjoyably, if you stop drinking.'

Again, substantial numbers of comparable statements should be developed.

These coverant statements are really condensations of anti-drinking thoughts, the kind of thoughts that we have previously described as aversive or punishing. They could be explained as reflecting various feelings, ideas and possibilities in relation to the present and future prospects of the drinker, prospects that might motivate the drinker to abstain from drinking, and break the habit.

*Pairing the statements*
Each would-be self-manager requires about four anti-drinking and four pro-non-drinking statements. These should be written down and learned in the order to be followed in the actual self-management programme itself, i.e. the first anti-drinking statement and the first pro-non-drinking statement paired together in one coverant control sequence, then the second anti-drinking statement and the second pro-non-drinking statement in the second sequence, and so on.

*Working on feelings*
The originators of this technique point out the uselessness of taking the statement as a bald recital of intent, repeating it automatically, moving on to the second statement, and thence to the positive reinforcement, ignoring the actual feelings and events which surround the coverant process. Their instructions have always been to suspend immediate distractions and struggle to think around and through the self-statements one is making, using them as cues to bring up the real connections with emotions and feelings about the

drink problem which has motivated one towards self-management. The whole trend should be towards a consistent mobilisation of anti-drinking feelings, and their connection with self and others, rather than a simple repetition of the statement.

*Anti-drinking fantasies*
There can be variations of the coverant technique. The consequences of heavy drinking can be very unpleasant indeed. A glance at the list of anti-drinking fantasies below will show what is possibly involved. As a change or supplement to the previous coverants we recommend coupling up such fantasies with the urges to drink, picking out the two most appropriate, and practising them by projecting oneself in imagination into the horrifying situations they depict.

1. You come awake slowly to find yourself sleeping rough in a derelict house. Plaster, bird droppings and bottles litter what remains of the floor. One corner has been used as a toilet, and soiled newspapers lie around it. You have an overwhelming feeling of nausea, but cutting through it is a steady raw ache from the right of your stomach, where the flesh is hard and unyielding to the touch. You roll over, and try to vomit, but you can bring up nothing.

2. You are in the Safety Officer's room, sitting unsteadily on a chair. In front of you are the Managing Director, the Safety Officer, the Works Convener, and someone in a raincoat you cannot place – he might be a policeman. The Safety Officer is speaking
   'Did you lock off the securing arm, or didn't you? Well did you or didn't you?'
   You mutter something about not being able to remember. You *can't* remember. It's all a fog.
   The Works Convener is speaking. He's defensive and sounds worried.
   'You can see he isn't well, can't you?' he says. 'I don't think he should be asked to prejudice his case, if he isn't well.'
   The Managing Director says, 'I can see he isn't well, but we've got two operators killed and one in intensive care.'

3. You are alive after the crash, but only just. You are, as far as you know, and you don't know much, in a ditch. There is water, cold dirty water half way up your legs. Your mouth is full of powdered glass; out of one eye, you can see the pulverised

remains of the speedometer. A voice says, 'This one's alive.' ...
'Bloody lucky,' says another voice. There is a great deal of
grinding and wrenching. 'Smells like a distillery,' says the first
voice. 'Pissed up to the bloody eyes,' says the other.

## 5. Activities and interests

If a sufferer can be drawn into supportive activities, and then, via
**leisure counselling**, encouraged to develop corresponding interests,
this programme will be substantially reinforced. There are several
useful activities possible for alcoholics, provided they have medical
clearance; perhaps the most appropriate is sessional swimming. A
number of advantages of swimming have been identified, including:

- The sessional swimmer may recover his/her sleeping rhythms.

- The bath's environment deprives the sessional swimmer alcoholic
  of stimuli to drink.

As emphasised in the exercise to follow, this is *not* a full list, and
more advantages can be added. Leisure counselling is a very
powerful tool to open advantages into interests. Such interests may
develop outside the context of, but be originated by, the specialised
advantages that swimming gives the alcoholic.

## EXERCISE 9.3

(a)  Identify at least another *six* separate advantages of swimming
     as an activity for the alcoholic.

(b)  Create a potential further counter-drinking interest from each
     of these advantages.

*Example*

| | |
|---|---|
| Swimming is genuinely appetite-building, and thus aversive to drinking which 'satisfies' hunger only artificially. | It may be possible to create an interest in cookery from this increase in genuine appetite, and thus produce a significant life-change. |

# 10
# Deciding in an Emergency

> Be prepared,
> That's the Boy Scouts'
> Marching song.
> Be prepared,
> As through life
> You march along.

*Tom Lehrer*

It's good to sing along with Tom Lehrer, and enjoy his cruel, kindly wit and his inimitable tunes, but perhaps we should also, occasionally, ponder on the useful truths his satire contains. Do we, in fact, need to be prepared as we march through life, and how much preparation should we do?

## REHEARSING FOR SPECIFIC EMERGENCIES

It would be fair to assume that most of humankind is not preoccupied with what it might or ought to do in an emergency. Most people do not, in fact, trouble until such time as trouble troubles them. They live their lives as if disasters were ordained to happen to someone else. Such **denial** seems to be a commonplace phenomenon, and in some circumstances can promote a negative attitude and non-compliance with benevolently intended safety precautions.

### Responding to unexpected challenges
And yet the average life is not as devoid of emergency happenings and the necessity to respond to them as commonly supposed. It has been calculated that in a normal lifetime, we may expect to have to respond to at least three emergencies. So, how do people shape up to such unexpected challenges when they occur?

The answer is, variously. Some, not many, behave magnificently, displaying not only exemplary calm, a passive but valuable response, but also the most ingenious solutions to terrifying dilemmas. From our own time, we have the quite extraordinary feat of the passenger on the capsized ferry, *Herald of Free Enterprise*, who bridged the chasm with his own body, allowing dozens of passengers to crawl over him to safety. Contrast this with the behaviour of the East End of London crowd who responded to the appearance of German bombing aircraft in 1917 by kneeling down in the streets to pray.

What generates this aptitude for calm thinking and calculated action that some personalities, often surprisingly, display in emergencies? The short answer is, we have little idea. Its most likely origin lies in early childhood, and derives from parental examples of responses to crises not characterised by panic or over-reaction. The difficulty with this explanation centres on the relative infrequency of emergency examples in the average infant or childhood as providing sufficient experiences. However, this might account for the aptitude's rarity; most personalities do not respond well to emergencies, because most childhoods do not provide the vital experiences.

### Understanding bizarre responses
Responses to emergency situations can be uncharacteristic, bizarre, even paradoxical. Held-up at gun-point by an armed robber, a hapless cashier in a bank handed over several stacks of notes she had been counting. The robber, clearly edgy, grabbed as many as he could stuff into a holdall, and made for the door. As he reached it, for reasons she could not explain, the cashier called him back. Equally inexplicably the robber returned to the position, whereupon the cashier handed him two more bundles of notes that he hadn't grabbed before.

The point about this behavioural oddity is that in circumstances other than armed robbery it is not an odd transaction. Both cashier and robber possess an overriding experience of the normal interactions of bank staff and customers. Take away the gun, and they become normal people but the gun is not sufficient to stifle entirely their normal behaviour.

And yet it is the case that **'normal' behaviour in abnormal situations can be dangerous and self-destructive**. Continue to breathe normally in a smoke-filled room, and you will soon cease to breathe at all.

### Being prepared
What this argument is leading to is the importance of being able to make good decisions in an emergency, because we are to some

extent prepared. There is nothing to beat personal experience for
distinguishing between prepared and unprepared situations, as the
following case history shows.


## CASE HISTORY: I AM BOTH FOREWARNED AND TAKEN UNAWARES

### Coping with disturbed sleep

Several years ago, accompanied by my family, I checked into a
large, crowded hotel in the Lake District. The place had been
disconcertingly modernised since my wife and I had stayed there
twenty years earlier, just before our wedding. Overpoweringly lavish
bars had been introduced, and television sets encumbered every
bedroom. These unwelcome innovations made me wary, and my
main preoccupation was with fire. I checked our bedroom window
access; it was a sheer drop of thirty feet. The fire instructions told
me to assemble in the main lounge, two floors down, if the alarm
bells sounded. I carefully laid out my car keys and valuables on the
dressing table, hung up a pair of trousers and readied a pullover.
Then my wife and I turned in, as did our elder son in another part
of the hotel.

At 2.00am or thereabouts the fire alarm sounded. Switching on
an easily located light, I grabbed my clothes and valuables, and,
together with my wife, was amongst the first to arrive at the
assembly point downstairs, where our son joined us.

After some minutes, the under-manager arrived. He informed the
remarkably small number of assembled guests that this was a false
alarm. He accused a sprawling guest in the adjoining bar (later
identified as a member of a well-known rugby club) of setting off the
alarm, and was answered in a spirited manner! We all set off back to
bed.

At four o'clock, the alarm went off again. 'This is it,' I said to
myself. 'This is the real one, and those who believe it to be a second
false alarm will be burned to death.' I trooped down to the assembly
point with my family. There was a bare handful this time; the under-
manager did not appear.

Despite a night to remember, and a breakfast to forget (another
member of the rugby club staggered into the dining room and
vomited on the carpet) I was filled with that complacent bonhomie
which is the reward of those who have not been caught napping. I
was uncharacteristically gracious to the grovelling manager as I and
about fifty other guests gathered at reception to settle our bills.

'Everybody gets that kind of guest from time to time,' I remember saying, consolingly. My mood even survived the discovery that during the night somebody had smashed an egg across the windscreen of my Vauxhall!

## Panicking in the street

But I can behave very differently in other circumstances. About two years after these events, my wife and I were wakened in the middle of the night at home by a noise. It was an odd, humming, hammering sort of noise, coming from nowhere in particular, but getting gradually louder. My wife, sons and I rose and scouted round, hearing the noise everywhere but being unable to locate its source. Finally, I went out of the front door, and there, under a street lamp, not five feet from my own gate, I saw the source. It was a burst water-main. The column of water rose a foot high, and already the hole it was excavating was two feet across. I shouted (waking the next door neighbour), ran for the 'phone and dialled 999.

It was then that I found that Emergencies did not include water-main bursts! 'That's not an emergency,' said the voice. 'You'll have to deal with the Water Board.'

I was in such a state I could hardly handle the telephone book. When I raised the Water Board I made a fresh discovery. The repair team had to be assembled, was ten miles away, and would be along 'as soon as they could'. I returned to the water-main, but found naught for my comfort, the hole was widening. At this rate, I calculated, it could be twenty feet across within an hour. Fearful memories of the blitz, with burst water-mains creating lakes in the streets, came back to me. I tried to console myself (but not at all successfully) by the thought that such lakes had probably been bomb craters. A river of water was pouring down the avenue, creating a new lake at its foot where a century previously an ornamental pool had been located.

My house stands unusually close to the pavement. If the Water Board team did not arrive speedily the crater would threaten the house's foundations. I envisaged months of homelessness while contesting insurance companies battled to evade liability. I ran around frantically seeking sandbags, but found neither bags or sand. It would be a considerable understatement to describe me as panic-stricken; shell-shocked might be more accurate. I stood on my front doorstep, shivering with cold and fright, and making little moaning noises.

The repair team arrived within the hour, a creditable performance considering it had needed to assemble and travel. The hole, which had continued to gush an enormous quantity of water, had not significantly enlarged during this period; evidently my grasp of hydraulics was as shaky as my poise.

I, my family, and half the neighbourhood watched while the team turned off the main and filled in the hole. I have since become very good at spotting leaks and trickles in the road. There is unequalled opportunity; the local water company holds the national record for bursts and water losses!

### Analysing my responses

So, here we have two very different responses to emergencies from the same individual. The first was controlled, deliberate, unflustered, capable of overriding even the fooleries of drunks, mood-maintaining, a source of enduring pride.

The second was totally different; I was reduced to a whimpering ineffectual wreck of a man, incapable even of the tasks of using the telephone book, or going to the end of the avenue to warn those householders menaced seriously by the flood.

### Lessons to be learned

1. Even panic-prone characters like me can be made calm and resolute, provided we have *some* opportunity to anticipate our reactions to emergencies.

2. This opportunity does not have to be extensive; indeed all that seems to be required to establish the vital mental 'set' is a short period of reasonably immediate rehearsal.

3. But this phrase 'reasonably immediate' raises the question: What is the optimal time interval?

4. This is not an easy question to answer. Clearly, in the hotel situation, there are timely prompt opportunities; for example, fire instructions displayed on the doors.

5. But what about me, confronted by a fire, say, in my own home? Would I be as calm as in the hotel, or as shaken as when the water main burst, also at home?

6. That is a very good question. In fact, I did face a fire at home more recently (an electrical fire in a car which I accidentally started) and I panicked completely.

7. So, as far as I am concerned, but perhaps not necessarily for

others, it would seem that regular specific mental rehearsals are required so that an adequate mental 'set' is maintained.

8. But does this mean that people like me must be constantly reviewing our responses to common eventualities, perhaps on a daily basis?

9. It would be wise for panic-prone folk like me, who seems depending on some degree of proximate mental rehearsal, to perform our own regular simulations, if we anticipate any kind of emergency.

10. How typical am I? Probably not typical, perhaps part of a minority, if the calm assured behaviour of my neighbour in tackling the domestic car fire is a guide. He telephoned the fire brigade, disconnected the car battery, and pushed the vehicle out of my garage, safely clear of the house.

11. But will not this put a burden of anticipation on already jittery folk like me?

12. Not necessarily. If anticipatory thinking can be made into a routine, so that, prior to any risk-taking behaviour – even the most ordinary, like taking the car out, or locking-up at night – we rehearse our emergency responses, then there should not be a burden.

13. Are there recommended exercises to develop such anticipation routines?

14. The following frameworks will assist.

## REHEARSING FOR THE UNEXPECTED

### Everyday rehearsal techniques
Almost every day of our lives we entail some risk. We do not always identify it, and even if the possibilities it might involve are apparent to us, we often take no special precautions or think more than briefly about them. But suppose we began to think seriously about risk, and our reactions to the unexpected? What would be the best method of systematising our thoughts?

### Charting the risks
We could begin by charting and analysing one week's risks, with their precautions and possible rehearsals. A typical daily risk might be driving to and from work. Precautions could vary, and include a regular check, say, of lights and tyres, but also involve changes of

route to avoid specific jams. Rehearsals might be standard fantasy routines for safety-belt release, fire-extinguisher-grabbing, or emergency exiting, etc.

A second daily or, more accurately, nightly risk in the week might be locking-up the house. Here the unvarying precautions likely are the securing of doors and checking of switches and taps, with a special weather or lurker watch. Fantasy routines could involve the easy location of electric torches in case of mains failure, or the imaginary arousal of elderly relatives in the event of fire.

Such a chart and analysis would be a most useful method both of mapping routine risks, and projecting comprehensive rehearsal programmes. The chart need not be complex; a sample corner with two risk entries would look like Figure 11.

There is no suggestion that a chart such as this should be kept for more than a few weeks. The aim is unambitiously to set an anticipation style which will cover and maintain the possibility of considered responses to at least two different emergencies.

While we are recommending systematic approaches, this is an excellent opportunity to introduce the all-too-frequent phenomenon of the **panic attack**, which will then act as a bridge to consider the very difficult area of generalising responses.

## COPING WITH PANIC ATTACKS

Although panic is the general term given to the response which an emergency frequently evokes, there is a more specific form of panic that strikes without the stimulus of an external or obvious happening. This is the panic attack, **a spasm of desperate anxiety which suddenly and unexpectedly overwhelms an individual, and causes him or her to react in irrational and unpredictable ways**.

Paradoxically, though it is difficult to modify panic responses to an unexpected emergency, those who suffer from regular panic attacks can be helped, sometimes quite dramatically by simple cognitive-behavioural aids.

The psychological accompaniments to panic attacks usually take the form of fears of dying to going mad. The sufferer may collapse, or possibly run off in a distracted manner. The attack is of short duration; fifteen minutes is typically sufficient for it to peak, and then diminish sharply.

The sufferer should certainly **seek psychological advice and appropriate therapy**, but a very useful cognitive-behavioural prompt is the following checklist.

P = precautions
R = mental rehearsals

| RISKS | | DAYS | | | | | | |
|---|---|---|---|---|---|---|---|---|
| | | Monday | Tuesday | Wednesday | Thursday | Friday | Saturday | Sunday |
| Driving to and from work | P/Lights Tyres | | | | | | X | X |
| | R/Safety belt Fire extinguisher | | | | | | X | X |
| Other risks during the day | | | | | | | | |
| Locking up the house at night | P/Doors Switches | The possible entries for this risk are limited | | | | | | |
| | R/Torches Access | | | | | | | |

Fig. 11. Daily risk chart.

## Checklist for panic attacks

1. I have had an attack like this before, but I've survived.

2. A moment ago I thought I was going to die (or go mad) but here I am, neither dead nor mad.

3. This panic will go the way of all the others; peak, fade and vanish.

4. There is nothing in this panic beyond an exaggeration of normal body sensations.

5. I have a kit of thought-stopping, relaxation techniques – now is the time to use it.

6. All I have to do is to act, and wait.

7. As soon as the attack begins to fade, I shall start to think again about the task it interrupted.

8. The number and intensity of my panics is decreasing; perhaps this will be the last.

## Using the checklist

This list should be typed, and then reprographically reduced to, say, playing card size, so that it can be held surreptitiously in the hand, or placed inside a handbag. When it has been memorised thoroughly there is no need for it to be produced in a panic attack; just fingering it in a pocket will suffice.

It is instructive and therapeutic to realise that the card is not a simple string of cues, but a highly contrived and directed panic-limiting programme in itself. Point (1), for instance, reinforces the idea that the panic, though repeated, is not inevitable and certainly not disastrous. Point (6) triggers a set of panic-reducing measures ranging from immediate relaxation techniques to the ingenious tactic of catching a glimpse of one's normal-seeming image in any available reflective surface. Other points attach themselves to parts of a wider panic-control programme.

## GENERALISING RESPONSE

The panic attack which, in a sense, summons generalised response to events that have no external reality, also provides some guidance as to the preparation of a coping kit to serve in situations which are totally unexpected, but very real and immediate indeed. Such a kit must be easily memorisable, and capable of being reduced to a semi-automatic drill.

## A kit for anticipating the unexpected

1. Unless your opportunity is exceptional (exit, etc. temporarily free, attacker's attack diverted), **do not move**. Stand easy.

2. **Start to count** slowly to yourself. When you reach ten, and every subsequent tenth number, say to yourself, 'I am calm.'

3. **Breathe deeply**, and continue to do so (except if smoke is developing). Do not shout, cry out or say anything. To yourself say, 'I am calm, I shall come through' at the same number intervals as before.

4. **Stop counting, and think**. Prompt yourself by saying 'How can I come through? I must come through. I owe it to myself to come through. Others need me to come through. There is time to think; there *is* time to think.'

5. Say, 'What do I need to do? Can I do it? Is it possible?' Because first ideas are not usually best ideas, wait for a second idea. If no second idea comes, say 'This is what I have to do. I have to put more into it than I've ever done before with anything. I'm going for it.'

## THE ORGANISATION'S RESPONSIBILITIES

Up to this point we have been writing as though decisions in emergencies, and the various hints and schemes to reduce the potential risks posed, are the exclusive responsibility of individuals. But this is obviously not the whole story; individuals are not alone, they are very often set in organisational contexts, and these organisations also have to shoulder safety responsibilities. Individuals owe a duty to themselves and their families, but the responsibilities of employers, say, are of a different order.

### The moral duty of employers

Employers have not only a legal but also a moral responsibility to ensure that their employees respond to emergencies in a practised and sensible manner. Indeed such moral responsibility and the determinations it implies may be crucial in ensuring their safety. Slackness in statutory safety-enforcement combined with employee laxity means that employers must struggle to overcome dangerous safety inertia, and need all the moral force they can muster. Duties imply tasks, and a priority task for any employer is the taking of an audit of emergencies.

### Audit of emergencies

This is the task to be approached in a systematic fashion. Considerable creative input is required which can only be supplied from co-operative effort. The motivation to make it effective is also dependent on co-operation, and is best built up by bringing in everybody likely to be involved in emergencies at the earliest manageable stage.

The first task is to set up a **brainstorming** group, whose job is to identify and assess emergency possibilities. Such a group should have a demanding remit. They will be required to:

- anticipate emergency events (not necessarily the immediately obvious)
- illustrate these within the contexts in which they are likely to occur
- forecast possible reactions to them
- rank them both in order of likely occurrence and in degree of tackleability.

The challenges posed here are both creative and analytic, and mean that the brainstorming group cannot be unfocused and allowed to function on a slack, free-associative basis, but must be strategically directed.

Pressed and directed, a competent brainstorming group should be able to produce a **short, prioritised list of emergency possibilities**. The next stage is to bring in the expertise of training and security staff, if necessary with the help of outside consultants, to devise:

- structural and organisational **safeguards** against emergency events
- **simulations**, role-plays and training programmes to proof staff as far as possible against panic reactions to emergencies occurring in spite of safeguards adopted.

### Using simulations

Simulation is the general term applied to rehearsal, typically of situations requiring crucial decisions.

It can be formal, as in a regular fire-drill, or informal, in the shape of a preparatory run-through of a talk to be given. It can be technically complex – elaborate aircraft pilot simulations are an excellent instance – or dependent entirely on written scripts, as, for example, a play rehearsal.

It is always, by definition, a **model experience of reality**, never reality itself, and can as a model be stopped in process, have its parts emphasised, and be reversed if necessary in ways which reality cannot match.

Finally, and most significantly, simulation must not be too real for fear of negating its own training objectives. **As its greatest dilemma, it must be specific to the future situation to be useful, while being general enough to answer the possibility of variation in reality.**

What must a good simulation deliver? If it is to be effective, an efficient simulation must:

- **Be timely** – give sufficient time for the lessons that it teaches to be absorbed.

- **Be authentic** – possess a well-judged flavour of authenticity (the real thing) while not attempting to overreach itself.

- **Preserve a novel tone** – even though repeated, a simulation must *never become a routine.*

- **Give time for contemplation** – this is advisable for any form of simulation, especially the active variety.

- **Give structure for contemplation** – group discussion, self-exploration guides and meditation opportunities are all useful modes of reinforcement.

- **Be as generalisable to varied events as practicable** – while preserving special features, also build general strengths, e.g. panic reduction, etc.

- **Be involving** – the most effective simulations have interest and appeal in their own right, quite apart from their training function.

## EXERCISES

### Organisational suggestions

There is a wide possible range, with fire precautions very much in prominence, but we have chosen attacks on staff as one of the most serious, topical and underrated risks faced by individuals in organisations. It is recommended that this exercise be run in tandem with the audit scheme described above.

## Attacks on staff

The failure of community mental health services, together with the deliberate engineering of social frustration, mean that staff in face-to-face contact with the public are liable to attack. This is especially the case for staff fronting helping services where such service is likely to be selectively offered. No employer, however, can be complacent. All organisations have an image, which to some precariously balanced persons may be hostile. Any organisation imagining that its image is exclusively benign is deluding itself.

## Checklist for attacks on staff

1. How alert are you as to your organisational image? Have you got too big for your corporate boots? Is a take-it-or-leave-it, we-make-the-rules attitude showing? If so, your staff may be vulnerable.

2. Have you identified vulnerable members of staff?

3. Have you sought the reactions of those identified?

4. Have you arranged special insurance cover for the vulnerable?

5. Are the vulnerable agreeable to participating in a training programme?

6. Is this programme professionally designed?

7. Does it contain video-instructional material?

8. Are there opportunities for role-playing?

9. Are the simulations tailored to emergency systems in place?

10. Is an observational log of callers being maintained?

This is not an exhaustive list, and additions should be made as appropriate.

## Individual suggestions

I have already proposed an intensive domestic charting exercise (see Figure 11) which, if followed, should provide you with some anticipation experience.

Another valuable exercise is to take the opportunity given by news stories of emergencies to momentarily put yourselves into the situations described, and develop for yourselves a model for response.

# 11
# Making Considered Decisions

## LOSING CONTROL AND LEARNED HELPLESSNESS

Seligman, an American psychologist, has written at length on a condition he terms **learned helplessness**, a state of feeling completely impotent in the face of overwhelming events, of losing control over one's life. This is not a happy state – depression and a sense of deep futility usually accompany it. As the name implies, some 'learning' in the shape of a chain of demoralising and self-undermining episodes of 'instruction' is necessary to establish it.

Learned helplessness is not an exclusively American phenomenon. Attempts by several Western governments to engineer social insecurity as a concession towards globalist control have had enormous general impacts on their societies, and on individuals in particular. Neo-Darwinist policies have often produced a very accurate perception that for the majority, decision-making is academic – significant choices are largely made elsewhere by others and the individual is powerless.

At an occupational level such powerlessness amongst employees low in a hierarchy can generate disproportionate stress and anomie. Striking gradients of ailments that hardly bother the powerful but bring the humble down are a consistent finding in all researches.

As the individual's or, for that matter, the group's capacity to influence events diminishes in one sector, so compensation is usually sought vicariously. For example, with the growth of the one-party state (American-style) in several Western countries, the decisive value of the vote is much reduced and issues, once subject to democratic control, are decided elsewhere.

There should be no surprise then if community action frustrates plans made when objections or counter-proposals are democratically disallowed. At an individual level the imperative to regain decisional control, by focusing on life-space where choices remain possible, becomes almost a matter of life or death, so crucial is it not to 'learn' helplessness.

## REGAINING CONTROL BY CREATIVE DECISION-MAKING

Becoming aware of the ways in which decisions are constrained, and then searching for fresh opportunities to exercise personal choice, are key elements in unlearning helplessness. The following questionnaire will help you explore your own experience of loss of control and powerlessness.

### Audit of control loss

1.  How much decisional control of your life have you lost in the last five years?

    None........Some........A great deal........

2.  In what areas have you lost control?

    Individual/Physical........Financial........

    Occupational......Moral/Psychological.......Social.......

    Domestic........Legal........

3.  Detail the extent to which this has occurred in the particular areas above.

4.  What has been the consequence of this loss in psycho-physiological terms? Have you suffered from:

    Hopelessness........Depression........Anxiety........

    Psychosomatic illness........Physical illness........

    Habit increase........

### Audit of intent to remain control

1.  Is regaining control feasible in any loss area?

2.  If not, which of the following potential areas offers an opportunity to experience substitutional decision-making?

    Hobbies........Activities........Interests........

3.  If no current opportunities present themselves, are you willing to explore *past* hobbies, activities or interests with a view to creating new decisional experiences?

4. Set out your plan of exploration, using the Aims, Information, Evaluation, Decision scheme as a model.

## Alternative lifestyles

There is a wide variety of possible alternative decision-lifestyles, each capable of generating great satisfaction, with significant therapeutic value for the individual who can contrive them. Examples are:

- A man whose work promotion has been thwarted and whose scope of decisional responsibility narrowed, finds fresh decisional opportunity in local politics, where he makes a real impact.

- A young woman in a screen-dominated, fragmented insurance job joins the women's Territorial Army, Medical Parachute Battalion and discovers the meaning of decision in action.

- A retired man, dubbed too old for professional responsibility, becomes a trustee, with a specialist role, for a national charity and finds himself inundated with decisions.

- A woman carer whose cared-for husband, though badly incapacitated, insists on interfering constantly with her running of their home. By juggling respite help she manages to attend classes in upholstery, cordon-bleu cookery and car maintenance, thus giving herself outside freedom of choice.

- A young male shop assistant in a dead-end occupation takes a part-time coaching course and subsequently helps with the coaching of local football teams. He discovers that maintaining several simultaneous training programmes provides ample scope for taking decisions.

## ASSERTION AND TAKING CONTROL

Exploring decisional space outside areas of constriction in an effort to compensate for the emotional loss of powerlessness, is a useful individual tactic and one which can promote emotional well-being. But another tactic, which might in some circumstances be tried first, is to test the limits of apparent powerlessness by significant assertion. Self-assertion is *not* an easy option and assertion with others is hardly easier. But it is possible given judgement, timing and courage. There is a range of points for the intending assertive to note.

## Assertion checklist

1.  No attempt at assertion should be made without careful situational assessment and, preferably, discussion with a disinterested other party.

2.  The cost–benefits of assertion are crucial; risks of labelling, discrimination, rejection, violent response, dismissal, etc. must all be weighed. Some contingency plan or fall-back position for example, refuge, new job opportunity, is advisable, if possible.

3.  All things being equal, however, a situation which does not allow moderate assertion is unlikely to be tolerable in the long run.

4.  Assertion is *not* aggression; it is a verbal or behavioural statement of the human right for personal consideration.

5.  Assertive acts, being untypical and usually unexpected, need calm, friendly but firm explanations.

6.  Assertive acts need planning and some rehearsal.

7.  Assertive acts need timing.

8.  Assertive acts are not once-and-for-all statements. They initiate crucial changes in relationships and need to be consistently sustained.

9.  When assertion is welcome, or becomes acceptable, benefits can be considerable and accrue to all parties.

10. Assertion is only a personal tactic; it must not become a lifestyle.

## REASSURING YOURSELF

### Attending to the present

Jesus of Nazareth's quietly simple 'Leave the dead to bury their dead' or L. P. Hartley's beautifully complex 'The past is a foreign country; they do things differently there' are both sayings embodying a powerful, prescriptive truth. They urge us, from standpoints separated by two millennia, to put aside ruminations over things done or left undone and attend to matters of the **present**, where we have real leverage over events.

But superb as they (and others similar) are, the reality is that they are sayings and, like all sayings, easier said than done. We all too often seek to interfere with funerals entrusted to the dead and we sometimes blunder around in an alien past baffled by the strangeness that we find there.

## Being affected by the past

With our over-evolved memories, summonable at will, we possess immediate and unique recall. But the **past** has a will of its own. It is not locked down in some complex, instinctual storehouse as with other animals. More often than not it is making efforts to impose itself on the present, seeking reinterpretation, pestering to be put back in a more comfortable compartment. Our decisional past is no exception and may continually invite us to mull over choices made long ago, and reconsider their outcomes. It is after all in the business of revision for its own purposes.

## Understanding the past

Though the novelist L. P. Hartley is a whole dimension less-regarded as a moral philosopher than Jesus of Nazareth, his warning about the past, and its reach to the present, has greater realism and practical psychology going for it. Jesus commands us to forget the past; as simply done as that. But though some may manage this feat, for the majority of humankind there is no easy escape into deliberate forgetting. Most need a fresh understanding of the reality of the past; mere instructions are irrelevant. In fact, as Hartley says, the past is a transformation. It is a place where **different people** (though perhaps walking around in the present) did **different things** (though apparently similar) and what was done had **different meanings**. It is not a spot for superficial musings, or for time-tourism. It has its own context and rules. We cannot hope to understand it or, more vitally, become reconciled to it, unless we grasp this difference.

## Coping with the power of the past

But grasping the difference is not the whole requirement. We need also to be able to cope with the power of the past. Consider the following phrases, usually self-voiced:

- 'Things have not turned out quite as expected.'
- 'I hope I did the right thing.'
- 'I've had second thoughts since then.'
- 'What else could I have possibly done?'

These are typical of the aftermath of important decisions and can become tormentingly obsessive if they rouse doubts that cannot be countered, or pose questions that lack answers.

But, as Hartley says, the past is in many ways an alien place. **We are not the people we once were** when the decisions we took were made. More significantly, those who took them with us are different people too. Any new knowledge we now possess is absolutely irrelevant. We did not know it then and the fact that we know it now is simply fortuitous.

### Having grounds for confidence

But the alienation of the past is not the sole reason why we should feel reassured over our decision-making. There are other rational grounds for confidence. If we can testify to ourselves that the four processes of deciding, **Aims**, **Information**, **Evaluation** and then, **Decision**, were faithfully followed in any decision of the past with a purchase on the present, then we have a weapon against self-recrimination of great power. And if we can also add to this self-declaration the warrant of **ethical choice** so much the better. To supplement it we need self-evidence of the morality of what was decided. We can only do this if we can be sure that a proper balance was set between our interest and those of others, based on our knowledge at the time, and that we evaluated this information at the same moment and in the same spirit as any other part of our decisional action. **Coupling due process with morality and with our backs firmly against Hartley's wall of difference, there is no way that doubt can defeat us.**

SHOULD WE GO ON THIS DECISION MAKING COURSE, OR NOT?

DUNNO!

# Appendix
# Cognitive-Behavioural Psychology

This broad theory has underpinned the entire text of the book, but readers may not be at all sure what it means. Definitions are always inadequate, but it is valid to say that cognitive-behavioural psychology is a problem-centred method of looking at conscious mental functioning, with a focus on discovering ways of directly attaining adjustments in thinking, feeling and action.

One good way of gaining a clearer idea of the significance of a topic is to list the objections and criticisms that are made about it. As far as cognitive-behavioural psychology is concerned, the accusations can be summarised as follows:

- CB psychologists do not recognise the existence of the unconscious mind.

- CB psychology is reductionist.

- CB psychology neglects feelings and emotions for thoughts and actions.

- CB psychology is over-structured.

- CB psychology is too outcomes-tied.

Let us deal with these in turn, examining the distinct and characteristic contributions made by CB psychology generally, and particularly in decision-making terms.

## (a) CB psychologists do not recognise the existence of the unconscious mind

In fact CB psychology accepts the existence of the unconscious mind, and acknowledges the important part it plays in determining feelings and actions. It understands the complications that can arise if the unconscious is at odds with conscious wishes and needs, especially when too much attention is paid to it. It is ready to address the unconscious mind as and when necessary, and more significantly when it is accessible.

Accessibility is important. Usually the unconscious mind is not accessible, and makes its attitudes plain, or at any rate felt, only in symptoms or dreams. But, sometimes, an opening appears to its mentally concealed depths, and then ways can be developed to exploit its creative resources, or influence it in other ways.

One such opening, or rather, a pair, occur at the waking to sleeping (hypnagogic) and sleeping to waking (hypnaompic) states. These were described in Chapter 6. In these dreamy periods, especially the former, all manner of hallucinations, visual, auditory and tactile, may be experienced, and their imagery manipulated. Hints have been listed to enable those wishing to exploit their hypnagogic/hypnopompic imagery to set about this task systematically. Exploiting the Twilight State then could involve most of the points in the following guide.

*Guide to Twilight State problem-solving*
1.  Not everyone can recover this childhood hypnagogic and/or hypnaompic capability, but it is worthwhile making the attempt.

2.  Some preparation is required, both in terms of mental 'set', and an easily available recording method.

3.  As regards the latter, those who recover new ideas expressible verbally will find a bedside tape-recorder invaluable for note-making. Those whose ideas are in diagrammatic, mathematical or technical form must have paper and pencil to hand, and be prepared to rouse themselves completely.

4.  In optimum circumstances, those who need to get up to make notes will find that they can 'drop off' again without difficulty; particularly with verbal self-assurance/congratulation.

5.  To return to point 2, the mental 'set' is difficult to describe, but essential to establish. Repeat to yourself, 'If I'm lucky to drift into the right state (or be roused and temporarily sleepy), I'll see what my subconscious can make of..................' (try to frame the problem mentally in advance).

6.  When you enter the state, say to yourself, 'Let's try for a solution to..................' Give yourself plenty of time and reassurance. Say 'It doesn't matter if we don't get it tonight.

Tomorrow night we may.' Keep the problem in the mind's eye centrally. Don't attempt to suppress any associations, however. Try to manipulate, adjust, substitute and shorten the presenting images.

7. As soon as you sense a solution, or an unexpectedly useful semi-solution, rouse yourself. This is especially important. It's only too easy to lapse into a satisfied deeper sleep. Either record a memo with a tape-recorder, or get up and make notes.

8. Now say, 'That's an achievement. I'm certainly going to sleep now' and try to achieve deep sleep.

9. On rising, review your notes or tape and expand during the day.

10. You may discover that only part of the problem has been solved. This is the moment to say coaxingly, and reassuringly, to your subconscious mind, 'So far, so good. But we can go further. Perhaps, tonight? But if not tonight, on some future night? One thing is certain, we can go further.'

11. The Twilight Technique can also be tried in daytime nap periods.

## (b) CB psychology is reductionist

Reductionism, i.e. the belief that wholes have parts, and can only be understood in terms of those parts, used to be a derogatory term. Holism, the doctrine that wholes can only be realistically interpreted as wholes, held sway in psychology until comparatively recently, and has only just begun to lose its grip. But despite being labelled thus, cognitive-behavioural psychology has always been confidently reductionist, believing that handles on problems must usefully be small, and approaches to solving difficulties must be taken in small, graded steps.

Cognitive-behavioural psychology naturally does not favour a holistic (whole view) approach to decision-making. It recognises that, in some circumstances, detail may distract a decision-maker from making a reasoned choice, but believes that in most cases the advantages of a systematic and, especially, a problem-solving treatment of the facts presented, much outweigh the occasional successes won by intuition.

So, CB psychology recommends the decision-maker to unbundle the essential parts of a decision or problem choice. Optimal solutions are likely to arise out of:

- the elements of the decision being set down in diagrammatic or, if time is involved, chart or phase form

- each element being assessed on its merits as contributing to the decision.

What then are the most important, specific contributions that cognitive-behavioural ways of thinking can give the decision-maker? There are several, by turns specific and general to the challenge of everyday choices, but one of the most recent, and important, is insight developed into the so-called, 'Concorde' or 'Sunk-cost' fallacy. This describes the strong human and, perhaps, lower animal tendency to base decisions for future action on the degree of past commitment. When we say, 'I'm in too deep to quit,' or make similar proverbial-type assertions, which echo the predicaments of successive British governments with their investment in Concorde, for example, we are confessing to irrational decision-making based on historical sentimentality. Proverbs are usefully revealing in such circumstances, and it may be that Concorde fallacy is rooted in an over-generalisation of the attitude expressed by, 'If at first you didn't succeed, try, try, again.' In this sense, the Concorde fallacy is not a new discovery, because we also have the counter-proverbs, 'Don't throw good money after bad,' and, 'It's time to cut your losses.'

Old or new discovery is not important. What is significant is the fresh focus that cognitive-behavioural psychology can put on the *reasoning* process which should govern all decisions, but which in the Concorde variety is being sidelined in favour of emotions such as regret, guilt, nostalgia or inertia. Cognitive-behavioural psychology, as specifically applied by psychologists with a rational-emotive or reason-before-feelings approach, goes to the root of Concorde decision-making. Because it does not carry historical ballast it is free to direct the decisionally-compromised to face the facts and analyse chances on a totally dispassionate basis. It can even, if required, devise ways in which the decisionally-compromised can deal with the emotions aroused by newly applied rationality.

## (c) CB psychology neglects feelings and emotions for thoughts and actions

Psychology as a discipline has a tendency to fragment, and the cognitive-behavioural variety is no exception. Over the last thirty years a rational-emotive version of CB psychology has emerged which puts the strongest emphasis on thinking as distinct from feeling, holding that thoughts drive or control emotions, and therefore rational thought processes must produce positive, self-affirmative moods. The therapeutic version of rational-emotive psychology is essentially concerned with identifying, challenging and modifying those thoughts which lead to self-destructive, compulsive, depressive or fear-dominated feelings and actions. It is not interested in the origins of such thoughts, or their analysis. Save for their attribution, its concern is with their elimination, or a reduction in their power and their eventual substitution.

Rational-emotive therapy can be applied on a self-help or counselling basis, although the latter is likely to be more successful. There are many strategies for thought-control and/or substitution. Notable among these are:

- *Relabelling*, the deliberate attempt to substitute more neutral adjectives or terms for emotionally provoking thoughts or self-statements.

- *Counter-philosophising*, identifying classes of thoughts by reference to learned, maladaptive habits of thinking, e.g. the habit of over-emphasising response to events, 'catastrophising'. Counter-philosophising attacks such habits.

- *Straight-thinking*, the attack on dubious conclusions from shaky or ambiguous facts, e.g. imagining a slight or insult where the intent was not clear, and might have been misinterpreted.

- *Thought-stopping*, identifying trains of self-derogatory thinking, either event-responsive or automatic, which can and should be stopped before they rouse inappropriate feelings.

- *Positive thinking practice*, the most forceful emphasis on positive, plentiful thinking. This is usually programmed as 'homework', but in fact the client is required to think positively in every working moment, and reward himself/herself for excluding negative thoughts.

The anti-drinking programme in Chapter 8 is an excellent example of cognitive-behavioural psychology in broad action, and also contains several typical rational-emotive contributions in thought stopping and control.

### (d) CB psychology is over-directive

CB psychology holds that, by definition, any problem serious enough to stimulate an appeal for help is unlikely to be solved by the seeker without substantial guidance. It does not by any means rule out the factor of self-help, but considers that self-discovery, in the sense of working out an independent strategy, is unlikely without much lapse of time and consequent frustration.

The road to discovery and the tactics likely to produce results must therefore be directed, but with the total co-operation of the client at every stage. There needs to be absolute mutual agreement; for example, on:

- the reinforcing or contracting programmes for mood or behaviour change

- the changes in lifestyle habits, especially in terms of everyday stimuli

- the homework or practice of various relaxation, desensitisation or personal skill-building techniques

- the identifying of problem priorities.

All such agreements will seem over-directive to those whose approach to human problem-solving is:

– restricted to a demonstration of unconditional, positive regard for the client, *and/or*

– providing a context for the client to feel secure, *or*

– who fear being drawn into making value judgements via too deep an involvement in client's problems.

But cognitive-behavioural psychology is neither inhibited nor restricted thus, because it is client-directed in an absolute sense, and is committed to full problem-solution.

### (e) CB psychology is over-structured

If understanding a problem is strictly on an informal basis with little pressure to prioritise important elements, devise immediate or long-term solutions, or even map out the area of concern as a whole, then no obvious structure is apparent. Structure of a kind there may well be, but it will be out of sight.

But CB psychology needs structure to operate. Structure, in the shape of items like questionnaires, decision trees, protocols, thought records, schemas and worksheets, is essential, and no progress can be made without it.

## (f) CB psychology is too outcomes-tied

This objection ignores the essential purpose of the theory applied, which is not only to realise an outcome, but to make it possible for the value and extent of that outcome to be tested. In this respect, and perhaps uniquely amongst psychological theories, CB psychology is not afraid of assessment; it even welcomes it.

# Glossary

**Age-pyramid**. The numerical proportions of a range of age-groups, arranged in layers, and often, but not always, resembling a pyramid.

**Brainstorming**. A technique for generating ideas by encouraging group members to free-associate concepts without restraint.

**Carcinogenic**. An identified causative factor in cancer.

**Cognitive-behavioural psychology**. A psychological method, emphasising conscious choice and control, and employing learning skills in problem-solving.

**Compulsions**. Strong, sometimes irresistible inner urges.

**Defence-mechanism**. A compensating or shielding mechanism used to cover guilt to inadequacy.

**Emphysema**. Enlargement of the cells of the lungs, causing serious loss of respiratory efficiency.

**Franchise**. A method of licensing the sale of a well-known product or service with the originator retaining rights and trademark.

**Hypnotherapy**. An approach to psychological or physical healing employing suggestions of betterment delivered during trance-states.

**In-basket exercise**. A management training exercise in which the trainee is faced with a sequence of written decisions drawn from a tray.

**Janus-face**. Facing in diametrically opposed directions, simultaneously.

**Marine underwriter**. Insurance broker who specialises in shipping business.

**Masochist**. One who experiences pleasure from pain.

**Mindset**. Mental attitude in advance of action.

**Neo-Darwinism**. The traditional evolutionary theory of the survival of the fittest by random selection, brought up to date by organised selective processes. Usually transferred in meaning from biological or zoological to social or economic contexts.

**Obsession**. Strong, sometimes unshiftable concentration of thought or feeling on a single idea or image.

**Reverse-yield index**. Measure of the comparative advantage, *in dividend terms*, of gilt-edged, non-speculative investments as against risk portfolios.

**Suggestion scheme**. A method of encouraging employee creativity by soliciting anonymous ideas.

**Unconscious**. Thoughts or attitudes which, although influential, are usually not part of conscious awareness.

**Wish-list**. Ambitions, usually privately held.

# Further Reading

*Living Decisions in Family and Community*, Vols. 1 & 2, Chris Adams, Stuart Gagg and Graham Tayer, BBC 1974.

*How To Be a Better Decision-Maker*, Alan Barker, Kogan Page 1996.

*Mind Over Mood*, Dennis Greenberg and Christine Padesky, Guilford 1995.

*A Manual for Leisure Counselling*, Dean Juniper, Kirkfield Publications 1993.

*Successful Problem-Solving*, Dean Juniper, Foulsham 1989.

*Decision-Making for Schools and Colleges*, Dean Juniper, Pergamon 1976

# Useful Addresses

The European Association of Decision-Making
c/o Dr Peter Ayton
Dept. of Psychology
City University
London.

The Society for Judgement and Decision-Making
c/o Professor H. Arkes
Ohio University
Columbus
Ohio.

# Index